Also by Dene Hellman
from Indigo Sea Press

The 99th Reunion
The People Under the House
A House for Her

indigoseapress.com

A Broken Hip Episode

By

Dene Hellman

Clear Light Books
Published by Indigo Sea Press
Winston-Salem

Clear Light Books
Indigo Sea Press
PO Box 67201
Winston-Salem, NC 27114
The events and opinions expressed in this work are entirely the creation of the author and do not represent the opinions or thoughts of the publisher. The author has represented and warranted all ownership and/or legal right to publish all the materials in this book.

Copyright 2018 by Dene Hellman
All rights reserved, including the right of reproduction in whole or part in any format.
First Clear Light Books edition published
August, 2018
Clear Light Books, Moon Sailor and all production design are trademarks of Indigo Sea Press, used under license.

For information regarding bulk purchases of this book, digital purchase and special discounts, please contact the publisher at indigoseapress@gmail.com

Cover Concept by Dene Hellman
Cover design by Pan Morelli
Manufactured in the United States of America
ISBN 978-1-63066-483-1

This book is dedicated
to all Certified Nursing Assistants (CNAs).
Their hard work and long hours
for extremely modest pay
with little acknowledgement
keep today's hospitals
and health care facilities running.
Attention must be paid.

Acknowledgments and Comments

The first time I fell down, I was two-years-old and not very good at this walking business. My mother and I were somewhere in town and I raced ahead of her, subsequently fell and lay sprawled and bawling in full view of Main Street. Since I wasn't really hurt, Mother may have been primed to reproach me for my behavior, but a passing woman got to me before she did.

The woman leaned over me and said, "Laugh and the world laughs with you; cry and you cry alone!" It was an outrageous thing to say to a toddler and Mother was so indignant about it that she likely skipped the scolding as she picked me up. Forever after, she detested the woman who had admonished me and told the story so many times that it became part of the family humor.

I've fallen from time to time since then, but mostly got by with outcomes not worth talking about, so it was a wallop from the blue when I broke a hip from a fall that came about when hanging curtains. And I have a lot of company at this hip-breaking business. Research turns up international pessimism about elderly women who do so. Rehab/nursing homes need changes and our culture needs to get over an attitude that aging women are invisible.

My good fortune at having appropriate medical care and a loving family is on my gratitude list each day. I want that good fortune for everyone. If the wacky journal that I kept during the first months help a reader know they are not/were not alone in their miseries and dilemmas, I'm glad. At the least, my wish is that some will laugh with me.

Of course, I had the added situation wherein, from my wheelchair and hospital bed, I watched the incredible state of affairs as Donald Trump advanced to being a candidate for the presidency of the United States. At no other time of my life would I have been parked in front of a television set the way I now was; a good friend of many decades, Dr. Hughlett Morris, insisted that my ensuing book should be titled:

A Fractured Hip and Donald Trump

That didn't work out, but I acknowledge the rationality of his thought and thank Hugh for a careful commentary that caused me to take another look at my manuscript. Appreciative thanks also go to Dr. Keith Van Zandt, who cheerfully and kindly sees me through my senior years and who thoughtfully answered medical questions that I had while writing *A Broken Hip Episode.*

A big thank you goes to Shirley Schaper, who shared much knowledge about care centers that she had accumulated from many vantage points. Additional thanks are due to Dr. Liz Wilson for proofreading copy and for insights she acquired during many years of teaching nursing students. Marcia Meis and Dr. Paul Meis deserve ongoing gratitude and thanks for the plethora of books and visits that kept my rehab weeks from feeling like incarceration.

In fact, all of the friends and family members who contributed to my well-being during and after the broken hip event should know that it was their love and attention and capacity for laughing *with* me that has meant so much. It helped me throughout, during my hospitalization and recovery, and still sustains me daily.

Special thanks go to my daughter, Patricia Bartholomew, who deserves them far beyond any recordable appreciation. Her contributions to my comfort and recuperation—before, during and after the hip break incident—make so much difference that I wish she could be cloned and sent to everyone in circumstances similar to mine.

As always, my appreciation and a thank you go to Mike Simpson of Indigo Sea Press who is unfailingly patient and never says, "Why would you want to write about *that*?"

A Broken Hip Episode

Preamble

Up on the stool she goes. It isn't that much of a stool—maybe less than nine inches high—but it adds just enough elevation for the job at hand.

She is old, beyond eighty years of age, but time hasn't dimmed her determination to live a tidy life.

Actually, a life beyond tidy.

Whether this is due to some kind of obsessive-compulsive mind set or to her early years in farm country when twice a year her mother announced that spring or fall cleaning must now begin, it has left her with a recurring need, twice every calendar year, to clean and organize so thoroughly that she does everything but pull the nails out of nail holes to give them a good scrub.

Never mind that where she now lives there is no unrelenting prairie wind blowing particles of top soil into her house, her cupboards, and on to her rugs. She nevertheless must clean.

On this day, having completed the bedrooms, bathrooms, linen cupboards and laundry closet on prior days, she has moved on to the kitchen and its greater challenges.

She feels very well and has decided to begin with the white window curtains. Standing on the small stool, she has removed them, then washed them and treated them to a hot iron.

Time to put them back. Up on the stool once again, she threads the curtain's pockets on their rod. Not a big job except one of the curtain panels balks at being evenly distributed. The rod, it seems, is just a little bit higher than she can comfortably reach and she decides that she must go to the garage for a step stool that will give her a few more inches of height.

Completely absorbed in her task, she forgets that she is already standing on a stool and steps backward. The feet are suspended in air and she sails backward in a slow motion arc to meet the hardwood floor. Even as this occurs, she knows what she has done and that the outcome will probably not be good.

Lying crumpled on the floor, she quickly discovers that she cannot move, that she has tremendous pain emanating from her left hip, and that she will be on the floor for a long time because nobody else is home.

"Help!" she screams, just like the woman in the commercial who has fallen and can't get up. She isn't surprised that nobody hears her.

Two or more hours later, her grandson arrives. An

A Broken Hip Episode

ambulance is called and the people who appear tell her that they must move her onto her back so they can put her on a stretcher.

From some far-off place, she hears herself screaming as they do so, but it is a sound that is unfamiliar. So intense is the pain that engulfs every fiber of her being that if ever in her prior life she has made that sound, it must have been while giving birth to one of her children.

September 9-10

My grandson rode up front with the ambulance driver. He left a note back at the house to inform his mother where we have gone and why. I remember that, as well as replying to a question about which of our town's hospitals we should access.

I remember being taken from the ambulance to the emergency entrance.

I remember that soon my daughter arrived.

I remember that, in due time, I was told that I had to be x-rayed and again emitting those animal screams at an incredible volume when I am moved onto the table in the x-ray room.

My left hip is broken in a sort of free-lance design that in no way resembles the neat pattern used when a hip is undergoing replacement. Do I know this because someone showed me the x-rays?

No, because my daughter is at my side and there must be an understanding that at this time she speaks for me. Who would consult with or explain things to a person of eighty-seven? I feel anger but am too wiped out to protest. And, anyway, I trust my daughter to make good decisions.

A Broken Hip Episode

Of course, the hip will have to be fixed. However, there is a big problem. One of the two prescription drugs that I take is warfarin—a blood thinner that I've taken for years—and my blood is, consequently, thin.

If I were to be immediately operated on to fix my hip, I could end up bleeding to death. That's certainly a predicament and the only answer is that no surgery can take place until my blood is at a normal, unthinned viscosity.

How long will that take? It is Thursday evening now so there will be no surgery tomorrow, which is Friday, and the coming weekend creates a problem.

The hospital staff continues to test my blood. Friday passes and on Saturday morning I have still not met a blood level standard that satisfies the surgeons who will operate.

By Saturday evening things are looking up. Sunday morning surgeries are certainly not the norm but I will be an exception.

How did I pass those days from Thursday evening until Sunday morning? Pain medication. More pain medication. Even more pain medication. As each dosage wears off, I beg for more and each time I am asked by a far-off voice to state my name and birth date. I have no idea which of many habit-forming concoctions I am given. At times like this, who cares?

My birth name is not one I use in daily life and writing. But my Social Security and other official records say that I am Nadine Frances Hellman and that at this time I am eighty-seven years of age.

I hadn't forgotten that.

"Nadine Frances Hellman, 4-7-29," I chant toward the dimly perceived persons who will see to it that I continue to be hooked up to the Source, the pain meds that deliver me from evil.

Patty and I talk sometimes, when I'm up to it. Her three sisters, my other three daughters, have called and we must have conversed on some level. They all live far away, half-way across the continent, and are upset that they can't be with me. My hope is that I reassured them, speaking from whatever recesses of judgment I might still have, that on any given day of my life I miss them and hope to see them soon. Today, however, their voices are nice to hear but pain rules over every possible desire and there isn't a thing they can do.

Patty and I discuss my big worry—that anesthesia used during surgery might permanently addle my brain. There is precedence for such a worry. During his last years, my late husband came out of heart surgery with a severely befuddled mind that cursed

A Broken Hip Episode

his last years and made taking care of him increasingly difficult. Medical people didn't want to talk about it when I sought the cause. It would be a long time before I found out that anesthesia added to old age mental deficiencies was the culprit.

I don't want to do a repeat performance. Maybe my brain is still functioning well, but who knows? I've been known to forget a name here and there as well as an occasional item on my mental to-do list. I'm eighty-seven, for God's sake!

Going by some things I've read in the intervening years, I therefore determine that my brain will be better off if a spinal block is used to sedate me, rather than more traditional anesthesia. I tell this to every medical person within earshot and probably to the persons who clean the floor. A very nice anesthesiologist shows up and I most certainly tell him. He makes no promises.

"I'm a writer," I say to each and every one of them. This is not said from vanity, but to accentuate my need to keep the status of my intellect intact. If anyone responds to this, it isn't part of my recollection. Perhaps a spinal block is often used for hip surgery, but nobody says so.

September 11

Early on Sunday morning, they come to get me for surgery. Well-dosed with pain meds, I recall nothing of it. The surgery is done at an earlier time than they told Patricia the day before, so she isn't there to give me the benefit of loving wishes for a successful outcome.

She is a victim of the weekend lull that overtakes health care facilities, even big hospitals. In all of them, patients are fed and provided essential care but the niceties are missing. That surely is why nobody informed her that my surgery will be earlier than originally planned. It is a shock when she arrives and finds my hospital room empty.

Frightened and worried, when she goes to the waiting room that serves as a holding tank for the anxious family and friends of people being worked on in the operating rooms, a blackboard notation tells her that I am in surgery. At some point a doctor comes in the room and tells her that I had spinal anesthesia, as requested, and all has gone well. He is off and running before she can ask questions.

So she sits and waits endlessly, with no more

information forthcoming. The blackboard that indicates who is in recovery and can be seen by their family never shows that is the case for me. After a long time of continuous worry, she goes back to my hospital room and finds me there, out of recovery, relatively verbal, momentarily alert and free of the pain that has racked me for days. Swallowing her anger at the lack of communication she has experienced, she realizes that she has been a victim of the hospital's weekend let-up. While she is never going to forget it, she certainly isn't going to complain to me.

We talk but I have no recollection of what we talk about. It is enough for me that I'm not alone, that my communications seem to be, at last, coherent, and that I have this beloved daughter to hold my hand. Calls come in from my other adored daughters, flowers and a bobbing balloon decorate the room, and my world seems much improved. My weekend hell no longer has anything to do with me. I have what I need.

That first night, courtesy of my surgery and overlapping medication, I hallucinate in what I later understand was a highly creative performance. People I would have sworn were real came and went, communicating in original ways. (Did I mention that I'm a writer?) Later, I am told that the department's night staff was so well entertained by my hallucinations that they pressed their ears to the wall that separated me from them so they wouldn't miss a word.

Hey! Creatives take their audiences wherever they find them.

I never do see another doctor or surgeon. Perhaps they don't talk with patients after they do their skilled work. Presumably, instructions for my care have been left with the nursing staff.

All in all, however, I continue to be grateful for my Sunday surgery, everlastingly thankful that I didn't have to wait until Monday.

A Broken Hip Episode

September 12-13

There's still a lot of need for pain medication but I'm now alert to my surroundings for longer periods. The hospital staff confounds me.

This is what people look like?

After years of existence in my own day-to-day environment, rarely watching television, writing my books, socializing mostly with family and friends, attending a small Unitarian Universalist fellowship with a largely professional membership, I have now crawled out of the glass jar that has surrounded me for years.

And find myself in full immersion in today's health care world.

Day and night, strange people with strange accents, strange complexions and—sometimes—strange sexuality surround me. Except for an occasional nurse there are no Caucasians to be seen.

Bottom line: I am cared for, cleaned, exercised, fed and medicated by many very nice people who, in some cases, seem to have come from other places in the world.

I murmur as much to Patricia, who is startled by

my observation. She has spent years in the education community where such diversity is the norm and hasn't realized how out of touch I have become.

As pain meds become part of my world instead of my entire world, the hospital staff begins to look like individuals instead of a social order. One of my earliest understandings is that if I need anything, including being helped to the commode, whoever answers my light is going to assist.

The first time I bashfully sit on the commode with one of the department's young men in attendance, I have to rationalize it.

I think how many decades of my life I have reported to male doctors, been delivered of babies by male doctors, had my gynecological status assessed by male doctors, and faithfully followed the instructions laid out by male doctors.

So, if a pleasant and coolly objective young black man is now the person who is assisting me with my urinary needs, whether a diaper or a commode, who am I to get all mortified about it?

Since I insist upon getting to the commode when I have to pee, it's explained that even the very few steps to be taken require a special technique. I cannot—absolutely *cannot* place my left foot flat on

A Broken Hip Episode

the floor. Each move forward requires me to move it by going tiptoe. This is awkward and exacerbates my discomfort so, sometimes, one of the large young men literally picks me up and transfers me.

Since I am often awake during the nights, the night staff becomes as familiar to me as those of earlier shifts. One young African American man is so tall that he looks as if he belongs on a basketball court rather than in a hospital ward. He has a delightful personality set off by a rakish attitude and corn-rowed hair and I want very much to call him by name. I look at the identification tag that he and all other hospital workers wear hanging around their necks.

The name puzzles me. It is, most likely, of African origin and I have no idea how to pronounce it. African-American mothers have a way of reaching for the unusual when naming their babies.

"Snah" (rhymes with "pa") is my best guess as I look at my helper's identification, but I'm too uncertain to come out with it.

"How do you pronounce your name?" I ask, careful not to add that African names aren't easy for me.

The young man looks puzzled. And squints his eyes downward to the I.D. tag that hangs around his neck, displaying his medical occupation in large capital letters.

"C N A?" he says, in a puzzled voice.

Then he flips his tag over to display his given name, which is as Anglo as it comes. "WILLIAM" is what it reads.

That will teach me not to make assumptions. At least, not when I'm on potent pain pills.

A Broken Hip Episode

September 14-19

The post-operative days are almost delightful, premium comfort when compared with the three days of horror that preceded them. Pain meds are generous, my family is attentive, efficient and cheerful personnel surround me. I'm willing to colonize, to put down long-lasting roots, to bask in everyone's warm attention.

But that is not to be.

Hospital orthopedic wards are not, it seems, for the recuperating whose recovery is long term. There are too many evils like MRSA lurking just around the corner. And, besides, beds are needed for the newly arrived who have freshly broken bones and require expert attention.

Thus, on September 14th I am collected by seemingly anonymous persons who wheel me into a vehicle that drives a short distance. Then they deposit me at a rehabilitation center that Patty has found after a careful but necessarily fast search. I soon will have a private room, they promise, but such a room isn't immediately available so I will, in the interim, share space with another patient.

Not a big surprise.

I'd been in one of these rehab places once before, after long-planned-for knee surgery. Unfortunately, its facilities left much to be desired and my assigned room was a double, shared with an unfortunate woman whose health situation required staff working under bright lights at midnight. She had evidently been transferred from a hospital much too soon, and the midnight attention didn't help. She died. I was sad for her but had become sleep-deprived, a condition not atoned for in any way. Additionally, the meals were inedible and often included food I could hardly identify.

After the staff left trays of leftovers to rot away in the bathroom for two days, I asked Patty to check me out of the facility so I could recover at home with the help of a visiting therapist. I vowed, at the time, to avoid rehab facilities for the rest of my life.

But now I am in a rehab center again, although one that has better vibes—the Willows. Since a broken hip leaves no alternative to a full agenda of supervised attention, I know I'm in for a pretty long haul and fervently hope for a good experience.

Until a private room materializes, I am, for the

A Broken Hip Episode

time being, deposited in the dreary front part of an already occupied room. There is no equity in the arrangement. My bed is smack against the wall and just overhead is a fluorescent light with nondescript strings that, when tugged, cause a fixture over the room's door to light up.

There is a bedside table jammed up against the bed and just enough room between the bed and the door for a commode. Beyond a dividing curtain that shelters the room's permanent occupant is a "bathroom" with a toilet and a sink. I won't be using it. Nor is there a need to navigate on tiptoe. I need help just to swing my behind the few inches between the bed and the commode. There is no way to wash my hands and none provided, but Patty has left me a stash of moist wipes. Otherwise, there is a dresser to hold whatever possessions I have brought with me and a small space where my wheelchair will be parked—with me in it—for the many hours each day when I'm not in the therapy unit.

Patty arrives. A doctor stops by. I may ask for pain meds when I think I need them, he says. We discuss a heart murmur that I've had for decades—perhaps most of my life. I say it is a non-event. He looks doubtful. It is the last time I will see him and I don't know if he will oversee my health charts. From then on, my immediate medical attention will come from a nice woman who surely has a medical degree and comes from some offshore island outside the States and whose accent is often hard to decipher.

The first doctor, however, leaves a legacy. In deference to my decades-old heart murmur, my food at the Willows will be a salt-free special diet.

It is realistically expected that I will be incontinent, but I hate the idea and here, as at the hospital, the nursing assistants are kind about swinging me over to the commode whenever I ask. Until night time and a change of shift, that is. At midnight, after little sleep, much squirming, and limited prospects of controlling my bladder, I pull the light switch to summon help.

And am visited by a *Third-Shift Person.*

She is a professionally garbed woman who has exceeded the dress requirements for a CNA and in fact looks sort of like old-time nurses who wore white uniforms. Her identification tag is prominent and it places her in a sort of pre-1990s category when nursing-related jobs commanded deference.

I am sorry that deference is so hard come by in current times and I appreciate the lady's longing for once-upon-a-time days when one's effort to get to be somebody brought respect. Her achievement must

A Broken Hip Episode

have been awesome. But time has passed and the lady is now a *Third-Shift Person*, probably at her own request.

I come to know them well. Some are wonderful people who have particular reasons for wanting to work at night. Some, speculation goes, prefer to work with less supervision and the chance that most patients won't require full-scale help during late night hours.

In this particular case, with this particular Third-Shift Person, I explain that I wish to be transferred to the commode rather than rely upon my diaper. I may have sounded prideful because this TSP (Third-Shift Person) is quite insensitive about examining my underwear and announces that it is suspiciously damp and likely it is too late to avoid being wet. Nevertheless, she makes some effort to move me over to the commode and, while the transfer is awkward and painful, I manage to achieve what is, to me, acceptable results.

Back to bed. The light goes out and the TSP departs. She has managed the transaction without a smile or agreeable word.

But the night is long, sleep is elusive, and once again I need to pee and pull the string that makes my signal light go on. I'm not being casual; controlling my bladder is painful but, to me, essential; my wait goes on for a long time before the third-shift person reappears.

She is angry. "Do you know how many calls I have to answer in a night?" she snarls. "Go back to sleep!"

She reaches up, pulls the string that caused the light to go on, thereby canceling it. Then she stomps out of the room, her self-importance intact.

I am angry as well but have to acknowledge that I can't hold on to my bladder anymore. Pulling myself to a partial sitting position by clutching the bed rail, I allow myself to pee and pee and pee. How can this terrible paper contrivance hold it all? Evidently it does but my sense of dignity is an immediate casualty.

The morning brings pleasanter vibes. The first-shift CNA who is assigned to this room is one of the most dexterous and quietly efficient people I will meet during my sojourn at the Willows. In many ways, he is an enigma because his demeanor is quietly competent, much like that of a kindly physician. He gives me the best sponge bath possible, gets me dressed, finds some purple gripper socks to match the purple sweat pants that Patty has bought

A Broken Hip Episode

for me at Walmart, and moves on to assist the woman who dwells behind the room's dividing curtain.

I've caught a few glimpses of her as she moves around and she is very old and very beautiful. Her hair is long and white, her body slender, her demeanor regal and silent. Now, the man helps her get dressed for the day. Her clothes are simple but she wears them well. I hear none of the continual "thank-you, thank-you" comments that I tend to lavish on those who do things for me. Perhaps she is used to being waited on and considers it her due? Her lack of spoken appreciation does annoy me and I'm astounded when, after she is dressed, I see a look of pride on the face of our mutual CNA. She can't see it but I can and know that this kind man, who must surely have an interesting history, has taken pride in his patients' looking and doing well. That pride, coupled with his gentle touch and quiet smile, is remarkable. I will never forget it.

If my (sort-of) roommate knows more about him, she never comments or addresses a casual word to him. Or to me, either. That evening, when Patty stops to see me on her way home from work, she and I exchange the kind of animated conversation usual to mothers and daughters who find themselves in atypical circumstances. My (sort-of) roommate snarls at us.

"Are you going to go on talking all night?" she asks.

We do our best to shut up and from then on are mindful that we are unwelcome poachers on another's territory.

Patty is in for weeks of an unremitting merry-go-round schedule. A continuously thoughtful and kind person, she will now be tested to the extreme. A teacher of young people with special needs, she now fits in daily visits to me and attention to special needs of mine. As long as I am at the Willows, that will include constant laundering of my clothes, accessing my financial accounts so my bills get paid, handling the inquiries of family members who live in out-of-state places, and shopping for personal items that I need. She finds and purchases comfortable clothes for this new life of mine, soul mates to my new purple fleece pants, and brings food extras to appease my hunger, plus daily newspapers so I can keep up with our local, national and international scene.

She never complains or looks harried. I think she is a saint, but how can that be when I, myself, am so flawed?

A Broken Hip Episode

The next few days will likely be the most miserable that befall me post-surgery. I wait and wait for a private room to become available while stashed in this slice of a bedroom that lies between the reasonable portion occupied by the lady-with-no-name and the corridor that lays without and its unending traffic of health personnel, meal carts, visitors, people going to the rehab unit. The television and the lavatory are within the province of the original tenant and a curtain delicately shields them from me and us from one another.

One night, at some point in the small hours, I lose control of myself in a way that is totally unfamiliar to me and to my family. Using my cell phone, one of the few personal items I have in this transitory abyss, I call Patty and insanely weep and wail. The recollection of doing so is vague, mostly forgotten by the next morning, but an indelible memory for Patty.

"You were terrified and confused," she later told me. "You didn't know where you were or why. You were having an anxiety attack."

It's humbling, and probably good for us, to occasionally be reminded of our primeval selves.

On Sunday, a grandson and a friend, together with Patty, crowd into my tiny piece of a room. We make it work and one of them points out that my ongoing discomfort in the wheelchair may be because it is lacking a seat cushion.

"Didn't know it was supposed to have one," I say as I fidget and constantly try to rearrange my backside into a more comfortable position.

Later, I point out the deficiency to a health worker who quickly finds a pad to replace the one that should have been there in the first place.

"Aaaah," I say, marveling that the chair has become so much more comfortable.

Even so, I daily ache with fatigue long before bedtime and this will be a lasting state of affairs for the weeks to come because an alternative easy chair never materializes and the option of stretching out on my bed doesn't exist. Therapy pops up at unscheduled intervals, morning and afternoon, and therapy is why I'm here.

I anesthetize myself at all times, except when I'm in therapy, by reading and reading and reading. Patty brings me books and two dear friends, Marcia and Paul, begin a process of ferrying books to me that lasts throughout my entire rehab period. All these people have good taste in their reading material; gratefully, I read it all.

A Broken Hip Episode

And I cannot tell you the name of a single one of those books. Maybe it was a digestive type of reading.

a) Substance in.

b) Followed by unnoticeable absorption.

c) And out the back end of my brain where it gets flushed away by the currents of medical processes happening to me and going on all around me.

There is a lot of food, trays and trays of it, three a day abounding with meat, flat canned vegetables without a hint of seasoning, a slice of the terrible bread my mother called "store bought." This is good food in comparison with that in some nursing homes and rehab centers. I wish one of them had my tray this very minute.

Now I am told that I must eat as much as I can, which is not going to be a success story. Food and I have had occasional fallings out during the last ten years. Yet, I've never grown thin—at least not below a size 12; it's just redistributed to my middle. I've looked decent when dressed but never svelte. Certainly never scrawny enough to make my loved ones shake their heads in disapproval.

I'm not entirely sure that I'm not getting different food from that delivered to other patients but surely,

I reason, theirs is tastier or, at least, seasoned. In the real world, where my hip is not broken, this is where I would have firmly and steadfastly gone on a crusade to make the supervising doctor understand that I have been through years of dialog with many medical disciplines with regard to my heart murmur and it was resolved years ago that it isn't doing me any harm, that I can eat and drink whatever my excellent state of health permits, and that being well into my late eighties testifies to my vigilance and that of my doctor.

But I am not in this rehabilitation facility to critique the meals, or even to deal with pain. The significant target is to *rehabilitate.* Toward that goal, twice each day I enter the therapy room, once to do exercises that will, ultimately, allow me to walk and move—as much as possible—as I was moving and walking before I went sailing backward off a stool. Later in the day, I will be taken to the therapy room once again for something they call occupational therapy that will improve the rest of me—the non-broken hip parts.

These therapists—the reigning monarchs of the rehab facility—have determined that my arms don't exhibit the strength that I need if I am to maneuver

A Broken Hip Episode

my own wheelchair and otherwise support my weight with a walker and in an assortment of other uses. Exercises to remedy this are employed.

The therapists must be obeyed. The forty-five minutes-to-an-hour of each session call out for cooperation, achievement and the standards that my mother instilled in me from birth. I must, I must, I truly *must* do well is what I've been taught since infancy—that it isn't conducive to one's health to simply stay in bed and read. Whatever I am assigned to do must be done, whether I like it or not.

The physical therapist whom I most often see, Dana, is a pleasant person, more relaxed than some of her colleagues, and she is generous about engaging in conversation—a welcome respite from the silence that surrounds me so much of the day. My occupational exercises are most often directed by Nicholas, the pleasant and only male of the group.

As I work to move those parts of my lower anatomy that must be reeducated to what they have been for most of the eighty-seven years since I first learned to walk, Dana counts along with me.

"Twenty times, now, then twenty times with the other leg. One, two, three, four ..."

Early in our weeks of rehab work, I wonder how she can stand the boredom. Is this what physical therapists do? Count and repeat with an unending line of people who have fallen off or stumbled upon or been damaged by as many injurious insults as the imagination can conceive?

Becoming a therapist requires a load of study and experience; this I know and respect. Never, ever, in my rehab experience do I ask, "How do you stand the boredom?" I need this boring repetition, day after day, to slowly increase in capability, if I'm to continue living what is left of my life with any degree of physical competence.

So I engage in self-criticism for watching the clock, unhappy that its hands move so slowly during my therapy sessions. Where is my better self, the super ego that has always watched me like a hawk and permitted so little goofing off? Maybe it slid under the refrigerator as I sailed backward from my curtain-hanging project and hit the hardwood floor.

In due time, my therapy session is finished until the next and the next and the next. The charming and stylish woman who has the responsibility of getting patients to their sessions on time, eases the brakes on my wheelchair and returns me to my room. Wistfully, I compliment her on her fashion sense, aware that I, myself, look pretty bad. She consoles me, upbeat about my eventual recovery.

My piece of a room is not a welcoming place where I can take up my life so why am I in such a hurry to finish my exercises? The therapy room isn't luxurious but it sure beats this tight space into which I have been crammed.

It doesn't take long to understand the workings of my pain pills. While the philosophy of rehab, I am told, is that within the limits of practical pharmacology, one may have pain medication as need dictates, I try hard to be stoic about pain. Of course, I overdo it.

"I think I can get by with a Tylenol," can end in a hip that throbs mercilessly after a few minutes of rehab exercise. I confer with the nurse I have taken to calling "Angel," the one who is in charge of daytime medicine dispersal, and we come up with a plan that will put pain medicine into my system at the most appropriate and useful times.

No matter how much my inner disciplinarian frowns, it is a nonnegotiable fact that I have shattered my hip and it hurts like hell when there is no intervention.

As compensation, the surgical wound that occurred when dealing with the broken bones is already healing. Luckily, I've always been a fast healer and this is no exception. With no mirror, I can't see for myself, but the medical people who come to renew the dressing and review the progress of my incision sometimes wax lyrical about the speed with which it heals. It will be nice if the bones inside are following suit but it will be some time before we know their status.

"Can I bring you anything?" Patty asks, as she asks every single day when she leaves to go home.

"Yes!" I say. "Please, bring me a notebook and a pen!"

No wonder I have felt at loose ends, even with all the books that are at my elbow, courtesy of family and friends. A place to write down the words that tumble through my head is as essential to me as any other rehabilitation exercise. It's part of my DNA. To think is to write, just as it has always been.

Patty laughs. "You got it!" she says.

A Broken Hip Episode

September 20

Without planning and fanfare, it happens.

A man whom I have frequently observed doing odd chores shows up at my bedside one morning.

"Your room is ready. Gonna wheel you in there now."

I sputter that I have some belongings in/on the little chest of drawers.

"Somebody will bring 'em," he promises.

Before I can ask any questions, my wheelchair is propelled down the hall and stops at a room somewhere near the first part of a main corridor.

It's a huge room, one surely designed, originally, to house two people. A nicely made-up hospital bed stands at one side, definitely not hugging a wall. There is a bedside table, a small chest of drawers, a television high up on the wall, a round table with chairs—the kind of place where a family might eat—and a larger chest of drawers. It's a simple place, no decorator's dream, but I am enthralled.

My escort sees this and is also pleased. He turns on the television. "Anything you want to watch?" He is hospitable to the max.

"CNN will do best," I say, because it has that crawling message space at the bottom of the screen. I wear hearing aids but, even so, if a television is turned up high enough for me to hear, it is a sure sign that all the people in any nearby vicinity—patients, visitors, workers—will hear it also and undoubtedly cringe. Best not to have any sound, just the scrolling information that can be read.

A CNA arrives with my skimpy possessions and tucks them into the nearby dresser. Items such as a couple of tops and a bathrobe and the fleece pants that have been brought to alternate with my purple pants are placed in a closet. A closet! On hangers! I'll never again take these for granted.

No one else shows up for quite some time. When I cause the light above my door to light up, a CNA whom I've never met comes in to assist me. She pushes my wheelchair to the door of the bathroom after placing my walker inside and waits patiently for me until I'm finished.

A bathroom! All mine! My toiletries have been neatly set on the sink and there is a plethora of towels. The toilet is elevated for my comfort.

I survey the bed. It is the usual hospital bed that looks too narrow for anybody to sleep in, much less change position, but it stands away from the wall and looks tidy, with its nicely arranged bedspread and pillows. The bedside table is uncluttered and holds a little box that is destined, according to its inscription, to hold teeth that one has removed for the night. I don't have any dental plates but wear a hearing aid in each ear—so the box becomes my hearing aid receptacle for those times when I've removed them. Always, I am terrified that these tiny appliances that have cost me thousands of dollars will roll away into some unseen crevice. Having a secure place to put them amounts to a luxury.

Over the years, I have stood in many an expensive hotel room deciding whether or not it reflects the amenities I paid for. The satisfaction I now feel when I examine my very own private rehab room is comparable, proof that there is life after Hilton and it doesn't depend upon wall-to-wall windows and a mint on the pillow.

Leaning back in my wheelchair, I watch CNN scroll forth the latest news.

Eventually, the chic and beautifully uniformed LPN who supervises the CNA staff arrives and says, "I didn't know you'd been moved!"

Likewise, the therapy staff must not know because nobody comes to collect me for sessions.

Patty has to hunt for me when she arrives to visit.

It is a bit of a mystery but not a problem. A day or so before, I had confided my discomfort with my piece of a shared room to somebody who shall forever be nameless. This was a person who knew how to get things done without making waves in the ocean of orderly agenda that surrounded me. But I didn't know that this person could or would follow up and my complaint had no ulterior motive. And if that person ever happens to read this, please know that I am forever grateful. Nor did I ask the pleasant workman who suddenly showed up to wheel me to my new digs where he got his instructions.

I'm sure he knew all about it because I come from a small town where ordinary folks often know things they never bother to share with authority figures.

A Broken Hip Episode

Sunday, September 25

I have colonized. I know the drill. It seems as if there should be background music playing, "You're in the Army now."

At 7:00 a.m. sharp, it is imperative that I rise from bed and there is always a CNA on hand to make sure of it. I need help to get to the bathroom and to administer a soapy washcloth to those parts of me in need of a sponge bath. Never, ever, is the possibility of a real shower introduced for consideration, but there may be good reasons for this. It is never explained during the several weeks that follow.

And I don't ask. My depleted energy level has also depleted any ambition I might have to pursue traditional grooming practices. I use no makeup and eschew wearing underwear under my knit pants or a bra under my fleece top.

My wardrobe is new and quite unlike the jeans and tee shirts that I wear around home. Obviously, squirming into denim pants and tugging on a zipper isn't practical for somebody with a newly patched-up hip. Plus, the temperature in the nursing home tends to swing between tepid and too cool for somebody who takes blood thinners. If I had to be naked for any length of time, as in a shower, I'd be miserable.

And, wriggling into a bra is presently too hard to negotiate so if I'm going to be bare under my shirt, the shirt had better be opaque.

Patty has roamed Wal-Mart in search of suitable clothes for me and purchased several pairs of thick fleece pants with elastic waists. Most of them also have elastic around the ankles and I can't figure out the rationale for that one. Inevitably, at least one of the legs starts riding up and the elastic hugs the calf of my leg. As soon as I push it down, it begins its upward journey once again. At least the pants are cheap and abundant; there must be a lot of people who wear them.

There are two pairs, however, that I refuse to wear, pants decorated with comic characters and of an immense size.

"I damn sure won't wear them," I pout.

"Why?" Pat asks. "I've seen some of the high school kids in them and they are so-o-o cute!"

I suggest that no way, no how, do I intend to match my wardrobe items to that of a high-schooler and that I regard these as clown pants. It is as close to a disagreement as we've had in years and I try to soften my irritation by explaining that I'm trying to hang on to whatever shreds of dignity I have and these supposedly amusing pants are the absolute antithesis of dignity.

She hangs them in the closet anyway, neatly in a row with the other pants.

Daily, my practical fleece pants are topped off by colored fleece pullover tops that are equally cheap and easy to get into. Together they make up a costume that is perfect for the exercising, housework and lounging done by any practical woman, as well as for the population of women in nursing homes and rehab centers. I must have overlooked them during past shopping trips.

Presumably, there are similar items of apparel in men's sizes but I don't know for sure because for some mysterious reason I never meet a male counterpart during my stay at the Willows. There just have to be some, though; men aren't immune from accidents and illnesses.

After dressing, I am established in my wheelchair, and breakfast arrives. This is the meal that I find most edible. Cereal, juice, toast, a tower of what I am assured is scrambled eggs. When I'm finished I grab my notebook and pen and begin scribbling. CNN is turned on and the news of the day begins its crawl across the bottom of the screen. Too often, the news is a litany of tragedies. Yesterday's mayhem is often accompanied by video coverage of the event as it happens. How, I wonder, could a family member shoot footage while another family member is being gunned down or otherwise damaged? If they have the presence of mind to do that, I think, couldn't they have put that composure to better use?

On this Sunday morning, I soon am taken to the therapy room for a session to help strengthen my arms. I make a bicycle-like wheel go round for ten minutes; I rise from my wheelchair seat and sit back down using my arms and unhurt leg. I do it again. And again.

I have doubts about time spent making the wheel go round. It seems to be a favorite with therapists who are trying to occupy patients in order to get other chores done. That's just my observation; it would be rude to say so out loud. After forty minutes I am taken back to my room and it's still only 9:30 in the morning. I am asked if I want to participate in a group Bible study and I say "no thank you" since I associate Bible study with a fundamentalism that isn't part of my belief system.

In refusing, I pass up the only time in six weeks

when I'll have a chance to socialize with people who aren't health workers or my personal family and friends. The Willows is filled with patients, but they are often behind closed doors when they aren't in rehab. I prefer to have the door to my room open and each time a health worker goes out of it, I am asked if that's my preference. I've tended to be a loner for much of my life, setting myself an agenda that allows for little socializing during times when I need to get on with my schedule, but the Willows harbors a stillness that has begun to feel eerie.

I need to put on my hall light when I need to go to the bathroom. It is a tiresome routine. I put on the light; someone eventually comes and moves me into my wheelchair; the wheelchair is then pushed to the door of the bathroom and I'm helped to the toilet. At some point, I peer into the mirror as I wash my hands and observe that I'm a mess.

Hair; despair. There hasn't been anything resembling a shampoo in the two weeks plus since the hip break. Who wants to be a hag during medical trauma? Who can avoid it? Not a time to meet the love of one's life—but loves of one's life seldom pop up in such circumstances. At age eighty-seven, they aren't much given to popping up anyway and for a long time that's been quite all right with me. However, I'd like to be more presentable for any entity that does show up.

Patty comes to visit and says she will bring some stuff and give me a dry shampoo. Results aren't guaranteed but I'm ready to try anything.

The nursing assistants are nearly always elaborately coifed. These aren't hair arrangements that one can do oneself, so they must have hairdressers skilled in the art of managing black hair. Money must be spent and leisure time used. A few women have decided not to go that route and have very short and natural hair, a professional look that I admire and would imitate if I had curly hair.

I wish that I could ask someone about the elaborate hairdos. Also, I've seen Michelle Obama's photo many times and she seems to find coiffures that have no particular ethnic look but always come off pleasantly. What do other black women think about Ms. Obama's coiffure? I decide not to go there.

The favor isn't returned. My hair looks dreadful and is open to occasional comment by well-meaning CNAs who, I can tell, are itching to improve my appearance.

A Broken Hip Episode

The crawling CNN news says that Arnold Palmer has died. In some interview, he said that he's happy to have brought golf to the masses. Perhaps as well as he played, that's logical. The masses seem to have responded well.

Golf hasn't registered much in my life since my early twenties. It cost too much for teachers with families. Besides, I showed no sign of playing decently and could have used those arm exercises I'm now doing in therapy.

Well, at least it is a genteel hobby. People don't go around on golf courses whipping out guns and shooting one another. Nor do its spectators exhibit ultimate yahoo-ism in sight and sound, as they do in so many other sports. Trump happens to own a lot of golf courses but we'll ignore that for the time being.

More golf—less football. That's the route to civilization.

I take to worrying about the cost of my rehab stay. Every month, I pay a lot to supplement Medicare—a couple of hundred dollars, plus, each month. That means that my total medical insurance costs me over $300 a month, and there are always deductibles lurking somewhere around the corner. Since I am usually quite well, those deductibles add up slowly.

Since my fall off the kitchen stool was in September, a relatively late part of the year, have I already paid the maximum deductible?

Maybe not a subject to be thinking about now. It's not like I can cancel the hip break episode.

If I do end up with unpaid expenses, maybe I can bring it all together and repay some of it each month? I certainly can't get up and walk out of here because it's too expensive. I lie in bed trying to do the arithmetic.

Changing the subject, I consider television in medical settings. I never watch it at home but here I turn it off only after I am in bed. Mostly CNN but with little stabs at other channels. It's therapeutic, even though I can't make out a single word after the hearing aids come out and are encased in their little metal box. It's what many people watch every day and they probably know a lot more than I do from simply perusing the newspaper.

Now, when I've never in my life been farther removed from the daily world, I know what's up with the world. Am I compensating? Is this a cover-up for my retreat from daily life?

It isn't necessary to decide right at the moment. At last, I sleep.

A Broken Hip Episode

September 27

It seems nobody was shot in any mall of the United States last night. However, the news anchors are always extremely busy dredging up outrage because they have to keep the viewers from hitting the off button.

These days, I'm prepared for anything and always terrified that bad things occurred when I wasn't looking. Not having been one to watch television in the daytime, I am trying to get the hang of it. Obviously, I don't have the option that I had at home to just go dust the coffee table or reorganize the freezer.

Today, CNN reports that Clinton won 62% to 27% over Trump in some poll and there will be other statements forthcoming. I hope CNN is correct.

Just another day for me. Into the bathroom to clean myself up with one of my semi-sufficient sponge baths, then get dressed and into the wheelchair for my breakfast and forthcoming trip to therapy.

Back to my room. Lunch. After a while, a

different kind of therapy.

I'm in a rut. Also in pain, but today people with medication don't come to give me a pill.

Another six hours goes by and the only person to show up is the lady who cleans the floor and the bathroom. This place is meticulously clean and mostly it's the same woman who takes care of this room. Each day that I see her I greet her cordially and get a tentative nod. Ultimately, I figure out that she either doesn't speak English or she has been told that she must not converse with the patients.

I go on anticipating the pain pill, hoping it will arrive before I start hurting so much that it will take a long time to recover.

A Broken Hip Episode

September 28

"Trump touts his performance at debate!"

Rather unusual behavior, it seems to me. "Touting" signifies something beyond pleased self-confidence.

But despite journalistic opinion, Trump claims a win and also complains the moderator asked unfair questions and something was wrong with his microphone. For a moment, my memory goes back to the early days when I taught elementary school and had to deal with the aggravation or tears of one or another student who hadn't yet learned to lose graciously, whether in a spelling test or at recess ball games.

Actually, that didn't happen often. Most kids learn the basics of loss etiquette at home or from classmates. Trump obviously didn't.

This must be the secret to the man's successes: *always* claim to have won—and let it be known that it was against terrible odds. It—this self-promotion—must be done without hesitation or qualification and thus *has* to be a skill going back to childhood.

That's a man thing, of course. Women are pretty

much a different story but it might work for a few.

"I was holding back," says Trump of his debate performance. "I'll hit her harder the next time."

Wow. Another big play—"I was holding back!"

Why would he have done so? Not from chivalry or caution. If he *was* holding back, it must have been—as it would be for most of us—a matter of coping with the unfamiliar.

Um. My hair. I went to the Willows' beauty shop yesterday and my hair was washed. That's an improvement and the hairdresser was competent. One of the CNAs urges me to go the whole nine yards—highlights, maybe curls. I try explaining that highlights are too expensive for my budget. She looks doubtful. Possibly, she has decided that hair is a non-negotiable expense.

Actually, I look—stringy and limp. As it would have been described in the 40s, 50s, 60s, 70s, anyway, and in my mother's vocabulary. What happened to pin curls and the omnipresent bobby pins? Bottom line—I just don't have any vanity left after my recent move to invalid status.

Okay. But maybe my hair actually isn't less attractive than the afros and tight perms and back combing that have punctuated the years. I reflect some more and decide there have been only a few good hair arrangements for Caucasian women since the world began. Maybe braids. Bobs of most lengths. Natural curl with well-shaped contours.

Other ethnicities' hair is a mystery and I won't presume. Why wasn't our species created to be bald?

September 29-30

How did I sleep? The medical staff seldom asks, but my family does. Well, on a good night the islands of sleep are denser and the distance between them shorter. On a bad night, there are long periods of wakefulness and just as I drift off I am awakened to take a pill or to have blood drawn.

Why do such things have to be done at 3:00 or 4:00 or 5:00 a.m.? This question has never been satisfactorily answered. Somehow, in daily life when one is *not* in a care center bed, lab people do tests that satisfy our physicians. We are simply told not to eat before presenting ourselves.

Again the food thing. Wish things tasted good. I don't think it's just me but I can't check the trays that come out of other patients' rooms. I once asked a CNA if she ate the rehab center food for lunch and she nearly doubled up laughing as she shook her head "No." We didn't exchange any words.

Thanks be for the milkshakes that Patty brings me nearly every day. I'm aware that she has little time after her school day to take care of other demands on her life, and am grateful that she regularly stops to get those shakes. Sometimes, I think they are all that stand between me and total hunger. The food that comes on the trays is too tasteless to be eaten by anyone who isn't ravenous and I haven't yet reached that point.

In and out of the therapy room. We patients are kindly coaxed through our necessary paces by therapists who have gone to school for eons to earn the right to do so. The exercises are boring to me, who needs them, and I wonder what they are doing to the psyche of the therapists.

My wish for the day includes getting a piece of good national news and a piece of good international news. I'm waiting! I decide that immaturity is behind much of the misery that occurs.

Question to ponder: why did nature choose such a long period of immaturity In—especially—males? Until age thirty or later, I've been told. It seems like a mistake.

Did such immaturity evolve to maintain an eager faction of defenders/attackers in order to protect/enlarge village life? What can be done so young men are mature and responsible at an earlier age?

Why is my head always spinning with such untimely topics?

In no time, it's Friday and I'm in a foul mood all day and pondering anger management.
One thing we need: Less computer skills and more life skills!
Why are college majors in psychology and sociology the kiss of death for careers? We need both more than anything—an understanding of how the mind works and methods for "healing" society's problems. Instead, everybody goes off to study computers and the psych majors end up selling insurance.

My god, there are a lot of things that don't interest me, I say to myself as I switch channels, going from one to twenty-five, skipping athletics, cars, cooking, contests, computers and cartoons.
What would I watch, if the opportunity offered? Gardening—homes—animals—some fashion—news that changes from this obsessive contest for the Presidency—book reviews—profiles of cities—history—some films. Of course, it would be nice if my hearing allowed me to understand any of what is said.

A Broken Hip Episode

I seem to have turned into a disgruntled old lady. This is a luxury I seldom allow myself but today my mind continues with its wretched negativity.

I've just read that Millennials don't go for national parks like Yellowstone and Yosemite—all of which stand for beauty, preserved landscapes, refuges for wild life. Will these Millennials grow out of this disregard before the parks disappear?

They will age but who will teach them as they do so?

What is the world coming to?

Not that my generation has been any better, although we didn't have the option of staring, for hours every day, into cell phone devices.

I need for somebody to come in and help put me to bed. If my brain has an off switch, now is the time to activate it. Tomorrow is another day. As a matter of fact, tomorrow is another month.

October 1

No new tragedy on the television today so they replay the last one over and over as they await an inevitable new one. At least, I'm in a better mood. There's a whole new month it says on the calendar that Patty brought in and pinned to my wall. When one has been dropped into a sort of crater, which is how the Willows feels to me, it's beneficial to stay oriented. And this new month has to be an improvement over the last one.

Do we do that in our lives: replay the last big tragedy or near-tragedy until we have a new one to brood about?

I've known some people like that. They hasten their worries along—leaping from one to another. I pray that will never be me, and I resolve to do a better job of staying upbeat.

These Libertarians are affecting the election, says a pundit or two. Oh no. Let them rise to replace the Republicans on the ballot, but please not spoil a positive outcome.

How many times can I say, speaking to my inner soul, "Thy will be done."? Despite being raised on

A Broken Hip Episode

that sentiment, it doesn't strike me as a useful adage to live by. True for my present circumstances, as well. No use anticipating discomfort or awkwardness or any other negative outcome.

The therapy folks have experience and get to call the shots. But I add apprehension to exasperation about this order to walk on the tiptoe of my left foot. It's awkward and feels incredibly unnatural. There's no rationale that I've been privy to, just the instruction to do it. There's a rumor that the therapy world or the hip surgeons or whoever is calling for this pirouette may soon rethink and retract the idea—but it won't happen today or tomorrow or next month so I'm stuck with it. Who came up with the idea and why? I'm supposed to do it in the bathroom, as well, during the times I stand before the sink washing my face and brushing my teeth. Well, it feels unnatural and lousy, and I don't always do it if nobody is looking.

Certainly, I want to get well and walk but when I allow my foot to rest flat on the floor it not only feels better, it's hard to imagine how it could be negatively affecting my left hip. Actually, I'm amazed at how little conversation I've had with any medical entity since my hip break episode.

Since the beginning of civilization, there have

been beliefs that doing this or that is bad for the progress of one's health. I'm pretty sure that being told not to put one's foot flat on the floor if one has a broken hip will join the crazy list.

Lobotomy, anyone?

Or some bloodletting, perhaps?

"Thy will be done" has been a tradition in the medical community. So I can scream internal protests but on I must go, prancing on tip-toe, continuing this crazy ballet.

A Broken Hip Episode

October 2

When I began this journal, I thought to record, from time to time, miscellaneous thoughts about my medical predicament. However, as the television news—in the form of bottom screen crawlers—slides past, hour by hour, the presidential race between Hillary Clinton and Donald Trump often overcomes everything else.

Woke up in the middle of the night thinking about nationalism. Nationalism? Yep. Russia. The United States. England. Syria. Et cetera. As bad as religion for turning people into quivering belief systems with potential for destruction.

First, pride unfurls the flag just as world religions—each with its chosen Symbol—raise the specter of an Almighty God with tendencies toward vengeance. Patriotic defensiveness requires that a nation's boundaries must not be intruded upon—just as specific religious symbols often cry out against more liberal doctrines.

And now Trump, always rich, says that only he

knows enough about taxes to fix tax problems. What sense does that make? Elect a thief because only a thief knows how people go about stealing. Elect a murderer because only a murderer knows what makes people murder? Elect an embezzler? A drug runner? A child abuser—each because of personal experience?

So ends my weekend meditation.

A Broken Hip Episode

October 3

Living with constant news isn't such a good idea. The screen crawler now reports that storms are threatening the Caribbean. I find myself squeezing my eyes shut and praying "Don't let it hit them," and then realizing how many eyes are shut as the prayers ascend to a variety of gods. It will hit if the weather pattern says it is going to hit and a million prayers aren't going to make a difference.

For much of my life, I did shut my eyes and plead when confronted with a difficult situation. As time has passed, I've slowly realized that solutions don't quite happen that way but prayer transformed into meditation has turned out to be very good for recognizing where a problem lays and doing one's best to deal with it. Hope I'll find a way to deal with this rehab environment!

They weighed me today and said I weigh 150 pounds. I've been 142 pounds for eons, even during years when I was eating normally generous portions. "How did this happen?" I shriek.

"Lying around in bed," says an unsympathetic CNA.

And when will that stop? I begin to rationalize.

Often, my weight goes up a couple of pounds, due to chance. Let me see: I have some bulky clothes on today plus shoes. Add two and a half pounds for that, as well as a little more for the "laying around."

Those allowances add maybe five pounds.

Does my puffed up leg add weight?

Well, I can't refuse entirely to eat. I need the calories. I'm eighty-seven years old and as long as my clothes fit, who cares what the scale says? Of course, the kind of clothes that I'm wearing these days don't have much fit to them. The elastic in my stretch pants will accommodate a lot.

Physical therapy goes on. It isn't entertaining or overly taxing or challenging. It doesn't change much from day to day but, nevertheless, I must be meeting some kind of goals because the therapists hasten to write down data that—presumably—meets set parameters. My biggest challenge now is to walk prescribed distances with that left foot touching down only on the toes. The distance to a door in the therapy room seems far away when it is pointed out as my goal. The therapist affixes a soft slipper/shoe to my left foot that squeaks if I put too much weight on it and I stand erect with the support of my ever-present walker.

A Broken Hip Episode

1. Small step with left foot.

2. Bring up the right foot with a hop.

3. Small step with the left foot.

S Q U E E K
On bad days: SQUEEK. SQUEEK. SQUEEK.
If only I were allowed to walk normally with both feet, I'd show them progress!! Maybe tomorrow.

October 4

Last night, between the blessed islands of sleep, I made up a new rule: *Never try to obey a tired, resentful CNA who tells you to do something that you know you shouldn't do—and that your therapists don't want you to do.*

"Get up and put on your clothes," I was told at 7:00 one morning by a CNA who had no wish to wait on me.

I had to fight the urge to obey her, even though what she wanted me to do was still out of my range of ability. But I am and always have been a good girl who was brought up to "never put people out." Putting people out was a big no-no back in the day, particularly in the Midwest where I grew up, but it hasn't translated well to the last few decades when people tend to go after whatever they need or want, regardless of the inconvenience to others.

In this case, I continued to sit in bed while my brain said, "You CAN"T do what she said, even if you want to."

The woman stomped off, neglecting to leave me

A Broken Hip Episode

with a call button within reach, so sit and sit and sit I did until the corridor nurse and the CNA came back, both defensive for some reason. I decided not to pursue my indignation. Why fight when you can't even pee without help?

Anyway, these certified nursing assistants are the leaven that causes a nursing facility to rise or fall flat. Sometimes they are tired and angry and have been known to work back-to-back shifts, totaling sixteen hours on the job.

Nobody should be allowed to do that. How can the judgment of a person be trusted if that person has worked thirteen, fourteen, fifteen hours or more? Easy to proclaim a barely ambulatory patient able to walk to the bathroom alone. Easy to dodge the essential if one is the only person around to do it.

I am helped by dozens of CNAs. Most of them begin their shifts as nice people, although a few appear angry no matter what. A tiny percentage have power complexes and another few have ethnic oriented hatreds.

Being an old white lady doesn't guarantee good will. And there are a lot of old white ladies in these care centers. Not all of *them* are well-behaved, either.

Some are demanding and critical. I know that because I've heard their voices from time to time making querulous demands. This is the South and I worry that a few of them may have forgotten that they have inherited no ethnic privileges.

None of this is surprising but I *am* surprised by the CNAs who always smile, even when exhausted (at which time the smiles may become forced.) Wonderful people who are earning their angel wings.

The nurses who give out pills or direct several CNAs are similar to the people they supervise but often in a more exaggerated way. A blessed few know exactly who they are, act only in ways that fit their self-understanding, and exhibit no inclination to be otherwise.

I've learned a little about the politics of care centers: therapists rule.

Never complain to one unless it's about something that *must* be addressed. That's because she or he will tackle the problem and the problem will be replaced by more subtle tribulations that will settle over you like mosquito netting.

And don't evade the moves the therapists want you to make, such as persuading them that you've done ten whatevers when you've only done eight.

October 5

The vice-presidential debates were last night. I'd been put to bed quite early so watched in comfort. No sound, just body language, so my opinion will have to be based on physical and facial movement alone. There will be no extra brownie points for a candidate with a well-honed vocabulary or deft choice of words. And no preconceived opinion because I don't know either of them.

My impression: two relatively decent men, Pence's behavior rather defensive, Keane's manner more outgoing. Each looks as if he could rise to the occasion if circumstances found him in the presidential chair.

Observation: Keane maybe looks to be left-handed. Hasn't that become a sort of presidential omen?

I'm suddenly noticing sort of a general silent treatment from the CNAs. What did I do to deserve that? One person's opinion or misunderstanding can be catching but I can't figure out what this general negative reaction can be based on. I try to act "normal," whatever "normal" is and discuss it with Patty when she visits. Her reaction is startling. She thinks I may be overdoing my "niceness," the "thank you so much" dialog that is part of my persona as a little old lady from the Midwest.

"*Too* polite?" she says, guessing that maybe what I perceive as courtesy could be taken as being phony- or weak?

Egad.

I will pretend that I'm my favorite nurse, who definitely has both feet on the ground, is kind but never seems to be currying favor. I'll limit my expressions of gratitude somewhat. Act more banal.

Most likely, the perceived "coolness" is a figment of my imagination. Not for the first time in my life, I wonder how a man would act in these circumstances. Most likely, even a very pleasant guy would somewhat temper his expressions of appreciation for services rendered.

Being a little old lady is a delicate balancing act between bitch and blarney, that's for sure. And, of course, nearly all men, especially older ones, are used to having services rendered.

A Broken Hip Episode

October 6

The east coast is bracing for Hurricane Matthew.

That immediacy outdoes the "ifs" of the presidential election. I have to remind myself that I now live in a coastal state. Far enough inland, thank God, to be safe from hurricanes—but a coastal state nevertheless.

And grandson Patrick is in the National Guard, which means that the worse things get, the more likely he is to be in the middle of it.

Does Trump say that Hillary caused the storm? Or that something President Obama did decreed where it will go?

Can it be that, eventually, climate change will end up disregarding words, slogans, politics all over the world, plus the sociology of millennials, baby boomers, the veterans of all wars and the wars themselves?

It is conceivable that in the end there will be only one enemy—*nature*.

Nature will punish us for all our follies and wipe us out as having been an immense mistake, an experiment gone wrong.

    What does my shattered hip matter in the scheme of things?

October 7

Therapy over for the day and it's only 10:30 a.m.

My first appointment with my surgeon is this afternoon, a sort of cap to the week. I'm going to leave these premises! Will there be good news? Will it turn out that I've healed spectacularly well and can go home? Over my lifetime, I've enjoyed many situations where health problems were quickly resolved.

Later:
No. No. No.

The travel to the medical office is fine and I'm accompanied by Liz, a terrific lady from the front office.

I do not see my surgeon, only a youthful physician's assistant who doesn't come off as particularly well-primed for my appointment. He seems to have peered at the new x-ray that has just been done but doesn't share it with me.

This non-sharing of x-rays is a new one for me. Whenever in my life there was a cause for an x-ray, its evidence was shared with me as the doctor of the hour pointed to this and that, explaining what's what and the tactics that were or will be used to fix it. The idea, I've always understood, is that the patient is a partner in the healing process.

But this broken hip episode is evidently none of my business. Why are they doing this? My suspicion is that these orthopedic medical people don't think much of elderly women. Perhaps some of the elderly are not well enough to be advocates for themselves, but no effort has been made to determine if I'm willing and able to discuss my hip.

Whatever this apprentice doctor has seen, he condemns me to two more weeks of toe-down therapy, followed by *at least* a week of therapy with my entire foot on the floor.

Wimp that I am, I thank him for his time and we go to the waiting room to wait for the bus back to rehab. Liz is excellent company, which is fortunate, because it takes a long time for the rehab bus to arrive and, due to numerous stops, even longer for the bus to reach the Willows. To my astonishment, I'm happy to get there.

But not home until the end of October? I choke back tears and try to concentrate on something wonderful that happens almost every Friday evening: family comes by with dinner! We giggle as my Willows supper tray is carried, untouched, out to the food cart in the hall and then we gather around the table that is part of my room's furnishings and see what's in the picnic hamper that Patty has brought.

That hamper is quite old. Years ago, it was a gift from my stepson to his father and me. Pure genius, assured of longevity! It's woven of wicker and he thought of everything when he filled it with matching dishes, silverware and napkins. It's been used from time to time but for most of its existence it stays parked on the highest shelf of the laundry closet and ignored for weeks, months, even years.

Now, Patty has recalled it and is using it for our Friday night picnics.

"A thing of beauty is a joy forever," said the poet. I have no doubt that this hamper will end up serving at least three generations.

October 8-9

How now today?

Little sleep, but not much need for assistance during the night. Surprisingly, my leg feels a bit more normal.

There's a new CNA today and she smiles a lot, which I badly need and much appreciate.

It's Saturday and I'm told that it rained last night.

Yesterday's P.A. announcement that I must do "toe-down" for two more weeks was a great disappointment but, after all, I will be home by the end of October or, at least, by the first week of November.

"Bite the bullet," is what I must do—reconciled that at least I'll be two weeks stronger when I go home. The strength brought about by the therapy thus far has had good effect and that's something to appreciate.

Back to the running words on CNN. Was there ever a candidate's running mate who said he couldn't condone remarks made by the presidential candidate? Pence has just done that—in response to a report on Trump's entitlement to grab women by the pussy and do whatever else because *he's a star.*

Trump can't fire Pence so what will he do? This

A Broken Hip Episode

is another outrageous scene in a welter of outrageous scenes. Where will it all end? Will Trump be out of the running before I'm out of rehab? Surely, that will be the case.

I must be getting better—or at least sufficiently better that I resume an old habit and spend half the night plotting a future novel. Sometime after midnight I reach for my notepad, my pen, my glasses and describe the six characters who will be featured in this future book.

A sure sign that I'm serious: I develop half a plot. A sure sign that the Clinton/Trump campaign is getting to me: the background is politics. Not national politics, certainly, but everything I ever knew about small-town politics.

Since this is being dredged up from the nether regions of my brain, I must have stowed away a lifetime of cynicism about politics in general. Once, forty years ago, I ran for a position on a town council. The man who ran against me wasn't popular and he belonged to the same political party that I did, but he won by a large margin for no particular reason except that he was male. Oh, there *was* the matter of the photos that would be part of our newspaper and campaign poster coverage.

My opponent's poster came out first and I went to the same photographer he had used—the only one in business locally. I sat; I looked at the camera; I was corrected.

"As a woman, your pose must be different," the photographer said.

"How so?" I asked.

"Your opponent was photographed looking directly at the camera." was the answer. "But as a woman, that isn't correct. You should be looking off to the side—not directly at all."

So during the period of campaigning, my opponent's manly gaze fixed upon the voting public while I was seen staring off into an abyss that lay beyond the left shoulders of the electorate.

The whole thing was educational and I went back with renewed determination to chairing the women's rights group that was garnering plenty of local criticism regardless of which direction we looked.

In case I ever look at this journal in the future, maybe I'll actually write the book about politics. Or not. Do I even have enough time left in my life to write a novel? Might be more sensible to stick to short-stories.

A Broken Hip Episode

Hurricane Matthew is passing, leaving several dead in this country and hundreds dead in Haiti. What do we need with politics and wars? Nature takes precedence and provides us with all the drama we can handle.

The Trump debacle is approaching a sort of climax. Somehow, I now wish to see it to a grand finale—defeat at the polls. And look toward an eternity of movies, Broadway productions, operas retelling this story for years. My question: If all of us can see him for the disaster he is, why not the Republicans? Why did the likes of Ryan and McCain endorse him?

I await the learned books, as well.
Gone With the Windy
The Old Man and the Tee
Lord of the Lies

A personal note: after the book plotting, several hours of decent sleep with intervals of the third shift CNA getting me on and off the bedpan. I *must* get to the bathroom when I wake up. Then I wash myself—badly—and brush my teeth and am steered to my daily portion of scrambled eggs. I've arrived at Sunday and Patty will come. Otherwise, the wheelchair is my home and I must gear up for two more weeks of toe-hopping therapy.

A touch of diarrhea today, which means more in and out of the bathroom. I put on my light as required—and mostly I wait ten to twenty minutes, a half-hour, more. The CNAs can't get to all the "lights on" rooms fast enough. So, increasingly, I defy the safety rules and maneuver my walker until I can get to my feet and shuffle to the bathroom on my own. I am not to do this but when the alternative is peeing all over myself and my chair, I go for it—and hope to be back in my chair looking innocent when a CNA does stop by.

"Not much they could do anyway," I tell myself. "They could *report* that they were present when I fell but they couldn't stop it from happening."

Tomorrow is another week of therapy and less time spent just sitting.

Tonight: Presidential Debate #2!

October 10

The Art of Button Pushing

There is daytime button pushing and there is nighttime button pushing. They vary a bit, depending upon the CNA who is assigned to your room.

Your reasons for pushing that button depend somewhat upon you as a person. If you think other people owe you, you will push it quickly. If—and I think that includes most of us—you aren't someone who insists on continuous service, you will have moments when you entertain a fantasy of your assigned CNA popping up to say (with a smile), "Do you need anything?"

Nope. Doesn't happen often. People always need something, if only to have their waste basket moved closer. And there aren't ever enough CNAs for the ones who are there to go looking for chores.

So you hesitate and about thirty seconds before intolerable you push your button. You *must* get to the bathroom to pee. You *must* have a pain pill so you can make your therapy session useful. You *must* have help to get up off the toilet and back to your waiting wheelchair.

So you wait.

You may sit on that toilet for a half hour, your "help" light shining before a CNA releases you to the wider world of your waiting wheelchair. She had an emergency down the corridor that far outweighed your trapped state. If your legs are a bit short for your feet to reach the floor and you have been very uncomfortable, think how it felt to your two-year-old when you said, "You're just going to sit there until you go potty!" (Nothing more useless than remorse sixty years too late.)

Hitting the button in the middle of the night takes a certain desperation. You were asleep, but now you need a bedpan and it's what woke you up. You woke up so desperate that you hit your button more quickly than usual. If you hope that you're a big girl who won't wet your diaper, you'd also better hope for an efficient aide, as well as a corridor of patients who either go ahead and pee in their diapers or who have stellar sphincters.

After once waiting for forty-five minutes I finally had to say to myself, "Well, what are these diapers for?" The CNA, when she came, was apologetic. There had been an emergency down the hall. She didn't say what but her tone and my imagination called for scenarios that would grace a soap opera.

A Broken Hip Episode

Often, I have the same CNA. She looks older than most of the others, is quite overweight and has a little difficulty walking. She always comes promptly when I push my button and always has her white protective gloves and the bedpan at the ready. Somewhat of a juggler, she balances the bedpan on the flat of one hand while she rearranges my "in case" diaper with the other. I sometimes peer up at the bedpan and envision it slipping from her grasp as a shower of pee rains down upon my head. It never has happened and I am grateful.

The woman is an impresario of bedpans. In a symphony of bedpans she would play first chair. I suspect that she knew exactly what she was doing and was enjoying some private amusement.

Meanwhile, back at the presidential campaign and the second debate, that second debate that we can't forget, no matter how much we'd like to.

It's spooky quiet on the networks.

The candidates didn't do the perfunctory handshake. Hillary was likely so turned off by Trump's outrageous sexual remarks recently exposed on tape that she wouldn't have taken his hand under any circumstances.

What is it about Trump that seems to attract a

yahoo element? Calling all pundits. Pinpoint that strange faction and address it in public discourse, please! And today, Trump's vice president candidate, Pence, is holding a rally right here in North Carolina. What does he have to say? Nothing noteworthy, evidently. He attracts little attention.

There's a lot that CNN isn't reporting. Can it be that even the pundits are stunned into silence?

October 11

Hillary/Trump: The sex tapes still front and center. It looks as if real issues have been set aside with emotional controversy all-important. Trump's public backers almost *all* strike me as immature in mental capacity if not in age.

The media goes for whatever is obscene. How many times do we have to see "pussy" presented, with and without little stars substituting for the middle letters? Is the press having a sort of holiday from discussing real issues? Maybe there just isn't enough of substance connected with Trump to engage in any kind of intellectual discourse and "pussy" has a way of filling in the blanks.

Meanwhile, the hurricane has come and gone, leaving hundreds dead in Haiti and over a dozen victims in North Carolina and the rest of the Southeastern Atlantic coast.

Bad experience last night. A CNA who was quite a prima donna and certainly not in favor of honoring patient need. She seemed to think my application for a bedpan an outrageous request. I was ordered to get out of bed and (dangerously) teeter to the bathroom. I explained my inadequacy to stay safe. So then the bedpan was shoved uncomfortably and inadequately under my buttocks in a position that made the result hit or miss.

It was a miss and resulted in wet pads spread over the mattress and under my body, wet pads that stayed in place all night while I dreamed about how good a shower would feel, how much I needed one, and how unlikely that I'd get one. I've been in the Willows for over a month and have never been offered a shower.

Enough. A pox on her kind. Likely, they dissemble when they come upon an administrator and talk, perhaps, of their professional pride. But I'd be willing to bet that their kids and grandkids and neighbors know them for who they are.

I spend the remainder of the night reviewing headlines. "Republicans on the brink of civil war over Trump," said one.

"I will teach them," says Trump.

Ah. Again, who did the Republicans *think* he was when they chose him in their primary?

Four more weeks until the election. What horrors will we continue to see and hear between now and then?

October 12

They're still evacuating flood victims in North Carolina—with twenty-four deaths in the U.S. from the hurricane and hundreds in Haiti. Trump be damned. Enough trouble without asses like him braying about/against everything. Or is he more or less just entertainment while we address (ignore?) our other problems? What will today bring?

I have random thoughts apropos of nothing and certainly frivolous.

a) Women on television wear some terrible clothes sometimes. And what will become of hair? Since most things end up the opposite tomorrow from what they are today, will all this straight, non-fancy hair be replaced by "dos" so elaborate it will take an "artiste" to do them?

b) And some major manufacturers have put phones and washing machines on the market that end up exploding in suitcases, pockets, purses and laundry rooms. Straight out of the *Dilbert* comic strip.

Marcia and Paul brought a pumpkin donut yesterday from Dunkin' Donuts and it tastes like ambrosia. This food thing is getting me down. I can't recall having a piece of cheese since hospitalization. And I could dream endlessly about *real* bread. With a genuine crust. Warm from the oven. With a lot of real butter.

Patty has sent a request for an absentee ballot for me. Wherever I am on election day, I probably can't stand in line at a poll. I haven't been away from home (wherever home was) for this long since one of the summers when my husband was in the University working on his M.A. degree. 1954 or 1955? We usually spent summers living in an assortment of trailers and Quonset huts that were miserably uncomfortable. "Married students' housing" they called it in their efforts to contend with a whole new education phenomena—these older men, married with children, pursuing education. I met more new and foreign people in those summers than I would have on a trip to Europe. Mostly women taking care of their kids while their husbands were getting fancy degrees. It wouldn't occur to us until decades later that we were being cheated out of a future for ourselves, a future that our prosperous husbands sometimes disregarded as they courted the young women who would become their second wives.

Al Gore is speaking in Florida tonight. How long has it been since he was elected President and the conservative Supreme Court took it away from him? Surely, we will be spared that kind of drama in the future. Sometime, voters will become smart enough to do away with the electoral college.

A "home" therapist director, looking toward my return home, tests me for my ability to sit/lie down/get up from bed. Talks about me having a home therapist a few times a week after I'm released. I guess I did okay. Everyone mentions "age" as a component in my physical need but they do it very tactfully and I play the game, assuring them I look forward to total recovery.

They bring in the scale. 144.6 pounds. Better/closer to my "normal" weight. If I hit 142, I'll be back at home base.

Nicholas, the occupational therapist, stops by and says I need to practice getting dressed and undressed. We will do it here, in my room. He tactfully lets me know that I will wear my daily garb underneath it all and asks if I have anything in my closet that is large enough to fit over the pants and top I am presently wearing.

Aha! Yes I do and I reach into the closet for the clown pants that Patty brought me and that I rejected as an assault on my dignity.

We practice shrugging in and out of things and Nicholas offers suggestions. He has brought a device that will allow me to put on my socks without getting into uncomfortable positions. While in rehab, I daily wear gripper socks but I know in my heart that I am unlikely to do so after I go home; they take up a lot of room in my shoes and from now on I intend to wear shoes everywhere except in the shower and in bed. I'm leery of the hardwood floors in our house and will eschew sock feet, gripper or not.

To change the subject, I semi-apologize for my weird clown pants and explain that I have never worn them before and never will again.

"Would *you* wear such a thing?" I ask.

And am taken off-guard when Nicholas says that yes, he likely would.

I've been watching a teenager (or someone so young that she looks like one). She is stick-thin, with long hair caught in a pony tail, and wears skin-tight pants and a dark, trendy top. She lounges in my doorway, doing nothing.

Her cell phone rings. She answers. She comes into my room and, ignoring me, walks into my bathroom and becomes engrossed in applying lip gloss.

She lounges some more, picks up two empty waste baskets, and saunters into the hall where she pseudo-dumps them.

She lounges again.

She takes a broom and pseudo-sweeps the floor of my room. This is too hard. She checks her lip gloss again and goes out to lounge in the hall, broom put aside.

Who is she? In my thicket of real people, I can't recall anyone like her; she belongs to a world of strange people who populate the lives of educators and other entities who are charged with making something of young, unmotivated persons. If, unfortunately, this young woman is old enough to vote, she will vote carelessly but with lip gloss intact. Perhaps she will take a selfie of herself in front of the polling place.

I guess that she's here in the rehab center as a participant in some work-study program that uses a good-sized chunk of money. Somehow, I am repelled. How dare the people who have put her here neglect to provide some kind of learning/activity experience for her? I will take the CNAs, mean ones included, the custodians who work so hard to keep everything shining clean, all of the real people who work their asses off to move the broken ones like me toward recovery before I will seriously consider this nothing child and her nothing supervision as part of a viable program.

Somebody—good people, probably—must have considered her and her peers worth educating but more needs doing. These nothing children must be made to earn their lip gloss and cell phones and their dedication to nothing.

On the telly: Hillary says, "I'm the last thing standing between you and apocalypse." If she were running against a sane rival, she says, she wouldn't be going to bed at night with a knot in the pit of her stomach.

OCTOBER 13

Today's news as it crawls across the screen:
1) Hurricane Nicole is aiming at Bermuda.
2) Women are accusing Trump of sexual advances.
3) Bob Dylan won a Nobel prize for literature (!)
4) Once reliably red states are within Democrats' grasp.

Dana, my physical therapist, is leaving for a new job next week. May the Force be with her. She has done so much to guide me toward walking again. The therapists are all an impressive bunch. They make up for the bad food and spotty nursing care. Not that they make an effort to be "impressive." They are steady, non-pretentious, hardworking, kind, and willing to endure limitless hours of counting to twenty as their patients swing a weighted foot up and down or lift arm weights or navigate with toes down in ballet stance.

They put the word "rehabilitation" in the name of the place. We blossom under their tutelage and then return to our lives.

October 14

Since my teens, October 14 has been a special day with a kind of mysterious undertone. It started, I think, when a youth church group to which I belonged made a trip to a town where I'd never been. Of course, I'd never been much of anywhere, so the trip really was special—and then it was made more so when an older boy whom I'd admired from afar sat beside me and held my hand.

That doesn't seem like much on which to base a lifetime of feeling special on October 14, so maybe some other great things later occurred on that day of the year. I wonder if today will bring anything out of the ordinary. Superstitious?

Superstition aside, I believe there is some kind of power out there that occasionally comes into play. Will this power eventually be explained by scientists? Otherwise, it's Friday. The weather is okay; my physical therapy is over with for the week; Trump's poll numbers are sliding. I am reconciled to my continuing days at the Willows.

Actually, Trump's numbers sliding downward is, for me, worthy of October 14.

October 15

Nothing truly outstanding occurred yesterday.

It's Saturday but I guess there will be some therapy. The Jodi Picoult book (*Leaving Time*) that I've finished was kind of a stunner. Great innovation. I'll have to investigate other books of hers. And make sure that I continue to understand what makes good writing. I have written two books that aren't bad but I have more to learn. The book of short-stories that's on my computer at home is another challenge. The stories are written but I'm fully aware that they must be worked over again before I turn them loose.

When I'm lucky enough to connect with a really good book by whatever author, past or current, I finish reading it, then turn back to the first page and read it again—mindfully, this time—to see what makes it good. It's not Writers' Workshop in Iowa City, but it's useful.

Patty will be here later. What a wonderful person she is. I'm complicating her weekend when she has so many things to do but I'm grateful for her presence and must remember not to protest when she has to leave.

My phone was shut off yesterday due to a misunderstanding over minutes, so I must make a lot of calls today to my family of daughters in Iowa and Wisconsin.

Nice Hispanic R.N. did blood work this morning. Thick accent. Vociferous about Trump. He knows the dangers, he says, but says he's also entertained—for the present. We agree that it will be far from entertaining if the man should happen to win.

Question on CNN. "Is Trump employable?"
Another of the sort of dumb discussions that have become so prevalent.
I'd say that people like him *must* work for themselves. They're too much trouble to manage—by the people of the United States as well if the unthinkable happened and he got elected.

A Broken Hip Episode

OCTOBER 16

So Saturday has slid into Sunday but maybe it's the beginning of my home stretch. The last week of toe-down, foot-up, anyway.

Also—is this possible?—I fear that I'm turning against my genial life here. No sleep last night, or precious little anyway, and the reel in my brain is unwinding in contrary patterns.

First of all, I'm *hungry*. Who put me on this cardiac diet and why? I've never been on a salt-free diet nor one so bland, even though I've had good medical care for years. Today, while others may get a chili-dog, I'll be given a slice of white Wonder bread. Or a slice of turkey on white bread with fake gravy smeared on top. Vegetables all out of the can and cooked to mush with *no* seasoning. Never a green salad. There was a half-banana several days ago. Some of this has no connection to a salt-free diet; it's just plain bad.

My blood pressure is stellar, often better than that of the people measuring it. My heart has been declared strong by all docs, including cardiologists. Why are they feeding me like this?

Should care centers be privately owned? This one is and I suppose most of them make part of their profits by keeping food costs low. Perhaps I should abandon my "go along to get along" stance and raise hell—but who will discuss my diet with me? And would the kitchen be able to do anything about making it better? Increasingly, I send my trays back barely touched, dependent on the food brought in from home on weekends and the box of fiber bars that Patty tucked into a dresser drawer at the beginning of my Willows sojourn.

What about the people who have no loving and understanding family to provide extras? No authorities are visible besides the physician whose accent is so heavy that I can't understand most of what she says. I like her but my good will doesn't compensate for the language barrier when I need to have a discussion.

And why do the CNAs and others begin yelling and banging things at 5:00 in the morning—just the time when one might catch a few winks to make up for the gaps in sleep that occurred during the night? Didn't hospitals and care centers used to be quiet? Is it an ethnic thing, this screaming communication during the earliest hours?

A Broken Hip Episode

I feel bitchy and want to get up out of my bed and scream, "SHUT UP!"

And I again reflect that I haven't had a shower since last month, on the morning of the day when I fell and broke my hip. My pitiful sponge baths don't reach all areas. My need for clean socks isn't addressed often enough. Indeed, my legs are a flaky, scaly exhibit of neglected flesh.

But, definitely, it's time for me to count my blessings and button my lip. These folks at the Willows are as tired of me as I am of them—or so it seems. My call button is rarely answered any more—at least not until a good bit of time has passed. I've stopped putting on my night light and waiting for a CNA to come with a bedpan. Instead, when I go to bed, I make sure that my walker is within reaching distance so, humoring my bladder at 3:00 in the night, I lay hands on the walker and navigate to the bathroom. Nobody has given me permission to do this, but nobody objects. In the morning, I wash myself as best I can and dress in clean clothes that I've laid out the night before, with Patty's help. My walker allows my progression to the wheelchair and I devote the remaining time until breakfast to quietly doing nothing. Could I not do that at home?

Definitely, it's time to go. Communication is lousy. Does anybody else see how it is or will I simply have to take up my belongings and walk out the door one of these days?

Yesterday, I filled out my absentee ballot and Patty took it to the mailbox on her way home. It almost seemed anticlimactic to fill in the little ovals beside each name. Not different from how I'd have voted before the broken hip episode but now I could deliver a lecture citing what has happened, who has said what about whom, the idiosyncrasies of the presidential debates, each potential vice-president's characteristics—and, apropos of nothing—what each candidate wore while stating her/his case.

This afternoon, Patty wheeled me out to see and feel the beautiful fall day and we were treated to two full concerts by a mockingbird. I look forward to once again seeing the feathered guests that frequent the bird feeders at home.

October 17-18

My physical therapy goes on, transferred from Dana, now gone on to her new job, to an attractive and very earnest woman with whom I've exchanged "good morning" greetings for the last several weeks. She puts me through a series of muscle tightening maneuvers that are done lying down. They make a lot of sense and aren't at all distressing. Again, I am grateful for all that's been done for me and for the people who have coached me toward mobility. As far as I can determine, there is no cost cutting in the rehab area and a bigger and better facility is being constructed at this time.

Carol, the very pleasant woman who manages the Willows has taken me on a wheelchair tour of all the glories that are to be. I am aware that she takes her orders from the out-of-town entity that owns this facility and, consequently, isn't responsible for some of the things that make me angry. She can't expand the food budget, modify doctor's orders, or wave a wand over those of the third shift who take advantage of their power over patients. Not unless she stays at the Willows twenty-four-seven. At any rate, she is thrilled that before long there will be a bigger therapy room, better stations for the nurses, and a nicer dining room for permanent residents.

I am grateful for her friendliness and do not bring up my dissatisfactions.

About twenty-four hours until the third presidential debate. Melania Trump's CNN interview of last night is reprised. She said she tells people that she "has two boys at home." Her young son and—Trump. Trump is a boy?

God forbid, my mind goes immediately to the book (*Lord of the Flies*) about boys trying to survive on an island without any adults to supervise. If Trump had been one of those boys, he would have been one of the bad ones. "Boy" doesn't confer cuteness. Or innocence. Or sincerity. This Melania Trump is, like all too many wives, going along to get along. I've done it myself.

Her perfectly made up face sets off her nicely arranged hair and her model-perfect use of her body underscores a professional perfection that achieves what it must. What will happen after the election which—presumably—the Republicans will lose? The Trumps will link arms and move on to the sunset cleaving only unto one another and the good of the United States?

A Broken Hip Episode

Fat chance!

I don't wish this woman anything bad. I just want her—them—to go away as quickly as possible.

Last night, for the third evening in a row, I got myself and my bed ready, Except for taking off my socks, an acrobatic feat I can't manage, I climbed in at 7:30, leaving the telly on just long enough to get a good look at Melania. At 8:00 I take the pills my nurse hands me. Then, except for getting myself up at 12:30 and 3:00 to use the bathroom, I get lots of sleep. There was a funny vignette at some wee hour wherein the room light shone brightly and the figure of a silent but genial third shift person moved toward my bed.

She hadn't seen a light asking for help and time had gone by. She anticipated the worst and had a fresh diaper clutched in one hand and a bedpan in the other, prepared for everything. Rearing myself onto one elbow, I said, "I don't need anything."

She looked puzzled and I gestured toward my walker. "I went to the bathroom by myself," I said.

She went into the bathroom to put the diaper and the bedpan away and silently left the room. I added her to my gratitude list.

Many third shift CNAs belong on some other kind

of list but this lady deserves much and I hope she doesn't have to wait until Eternity to get it.

A Broken Hip Episode

October 19

The final presidential debate is tonight. What do they expect, to cause them to herald it so much? A raving Trump who does something so terrible that it will feed the headlines for weeks/months/years? Who's to say the pundits won't get their wish?

Water. What is more important to a convalescent? I either have partially filled glasses marching across my chair side/bedside table-all delivered on various meal trays, or with vitamin tablets—or I am without anything remotely fresh and cold.

I have a water pitcher. It has my room number scrawled on its side and from time to time—at ever lengthening intervals—someone fills it with ice and water. It went missing the other day and was absent for at least twenty-four hours. I asked for it—or for water in other containers—all day long. Whomever I asked went away to find it and never came back. By 2:00 in the morning I was very thirsty but afraid to drink the last from the water glass that I'd taken from my supper tray. What if I became even thirstier and had no water at all?

Putting on my night light, I'm pleased when the bearded dispenser of late night medicines comes. I explain my dilemma and he does two things. First, he brings me a glass of cold water. Then he goes hunting and is gone for a long time.

The water pitcher mystery had been his undoing, I fantasize, and someone will ultimately find him—head first—in a dishwasher that has gone viral.

But no, back he ultimately comes, my room number identified water pitcher in hand and filled to the top.

"Where did you find it?" I ask, leery of a bizarre explanation.

The answer *is* sort of bizarre. Something about pitchers being washed on Tuesdays. Something about how my pitcher had escaped attention and was set aside, perhaps awaiting some future Tuesday.

I swallow a long, cold mouthful of water and go back to sleep.

Theme for last days in a rehab center:
"I'm nobody's baby now. Dum te dum te dum."

I'm as good as finished here, despite the road ahead as I struggle to gather strength and agility. No CNA claims me. No doctor has come near me since my surgery except for the lady with a heavy accent with whom communication was difficult. Thousands of dollars have been applied on my behalf to the charges of various institutions for many services. Probably, I will never see an itemized bill. Now that I'm getting so much less attention, are the charges less?

Unlikely.

Soon, I will be taken home by my daughter and lovingly cared for. Eventually I will walk with little or no assistance, my hip outfitted with metal that, in company with my reconstructed knees, will set off airport alarms. In the meantime, home therapists will call upon me to help with walking skills.

Regardless of my complaints, I am among the most fortunate of people. My income is limited but I have insurance that draws caregiving entities to my side. Plus, my daughter is a teacher—not a profession that attracts much money but one that has mechanisms in place for taking family leave when it is needed.

And so.

And so I will walk again and work to resume my place in the family as a giver, not a taker.

My hair has been done! Recolored! Down with the grown-in white, cheers to Loreal! Apprehensive that a professional coloring will result in an unfortunate hue, I have agreed with Patty's suggestion that she bring in one of the Loreal coloring packages that are in my bathroom at home. We consult the Willows hairdresser, assuring her that I will pay full price for her services, and she agrees that, although it's rather unusual, she can use my home coloring kit rather than that in her professional supplies.

The process over, I am allowed to pretend to myself that I'm younger than eighty-seven. The CNA who comes to get me at the little beauty shop takes me part way down the long corridors, then says, "Okay. You can go the rest of the way alone."

I am terrified. Wheel my chair all by myself and find my room? But it's easier than I anticipate and I'm soon back in my room, my childish fears overcome.

After all, I am an adult with grown-up hair color and ready to face the next challenges.

October 20

"Good morning, Miss Nadine," says the nurse.

Wow. I feel as if I'm in the middle of *To Kill a Mockingbird!*

"Miss Nadine" has a nice ring to it. In the beginning of my stay here, I was "Mrs. Hellman." Then I tried to get some of the staff to call me "Dene."

Didn't work. They have no recognition of this "Dene" person because my full legal name is on all my paper work.

Now they have compromised, perhaps feeling they at last know me, going mega Southern as they do so.

"Miss Nadine."

Like "Miss Scarlett" or "Miss Caroline."

If they'd done this before, I certainly would have felt more at home.

The debates are over. Trump has refused to say he'll accept election results. Vice President candidate Kaine says that's irrelevant. Somewhere, I hope there are serious people with expertise and political experience discussing what should be done in the various eventualities Trump is capable of producing. What would Adolf Hitler have done if he hadn't been put in office?

Bad stuff. And he'd probably do it over and over until he got what he wanted.

Is Trump strong enough to do that when he loses the election, as he surely will? Is he capable of attracting enough of the powerful people of the future to his side so he will eventually get into power?

I don't think so but don't have a crystal ball. People change. Public opinion is flexible. The human animal is unpredictable.

Someone, eventually, might actually lift this terrible person into the highest office in the land. The thought is so negative that I try to dismiss it.

A Broken Hip Episode

October 21

The administrator brought her new puppy into work today. He's fresh from his plane trip of yesterday that brought him from Minnesota to North Carolina.

He has that bashful puppy look that's so irresistible. A beautiful border collie, he will soon, if true to breed, be full of piss and vinegar.

Babies of all sorts make people happy and I'm jealous. Will there ever be another dog in my life? My precious Maine coon cat, Chi, died a year ago and I've never stopped missing her. Since she can't ever be replaced in my heart, would a dog be a more likely household member? Patty wants a dog. Maybe she needs to be encouraged to overcome her worry that a dog would be too much for me to handle.

My thoughts are turning more and more to home but I want to remember all the nice people who have helped me here. I say their names over and try to write them down—the therapists and nurses and CNAs and the people in the front office. A funny thing has happened to my mental images of these people; I can't recall what race they are. Black?

White? Latino? I knew in the beginning but they've taken on the color of their dispositions and the degree of helpfulness they project so color is no longer part of their identity.

On television, there is a story about a woman who has died from a chiropractic treatment. Something broke in her neck. Ah, yes, the neck cracking thing. I remember it well and recall a brave acquaintance who refused to let her chiropractor do that. I recollect that he became quite incensed over her refusal.

There will now be hell to pay in the chiropractic world, but things will change and move on. As in all aspects of medicine.

We all look for help in easing our physical and mental woes, wherever we can find it and within the constraints of current medical conviction. We are then disappointed when things we have taken for granted turn out to be a fallacy.

Will the time come when post-surgical care changes? Will the rehab facilities of the future emphasize good food and social cheerfulness over routine care? Will the people with broken hips be spared walking on tiptoe?

There's one thing that this facility does; every

A Broken Hip Episode

Friday, well-behaved dogs are welcome to stroll the premises with their owners. Who can deny the luster they bring to patient morale?

A big charity dinner last night and Trump and Clinton were seated with only one person—a robed cleric—sitting between them. These "witty" dinners are set up with some frequency and arch rivals deliver well-honed satirical remarks. These are then laughed at most heartily by their opponents and by the television audience.

A weird custom in our civilized world but perhaps *civilized* is a true description. The remarks are, of course, written by skilled wits who are paid to be clever. The various politicos deliver their lines as well as they can, pretending spontaneity, and we are to understand that they, too, have intellects and that their cleverness sometimes allows them to soar intellectually above the fray.

Donald Trump's wife, Melania, whose English is not a first language, looks terrified of laughing at the wrong thing and only does so when she sees someone she trusts laughing freely. How on earth could she handle being First Lady?

Patty calls that I have an appointment with my

surgeon next Thursday. Will I still be here? I'm easy money nowadays. People may present bills for my care without having to give my care much thought. Now, in turn, the surgeon will consider me. For better or worse, I am supposed to be on the road to recovery. Opining on my condition won't take much time or trouble but will justify an additional bill.

This just in: I'm to be dismissed on the 28th and, since the appointment with the doctor is on the 27th, the rehab people will take me to the medical facility. Okay. Most things seem to be out of my hands and hardly worth a comment.

October 22

Not another Saturday! Yes—and another Sunday coming up. Hours and hours of sitting in the wheelchair. My *last* Saturday, though, and I am ready to break out if my dismissal is postponed.

A bad start to the day, too. Up at the exact time of 7:00 and into the bathroom, where I first perch on the toilet. A head pokes around the corner with "Good morning!"

It is the weekend occupational therapist and I am annoyed.

"I'm here to watch you wash yourself and get dressed!" she chirps.

Suddenly, I am angry. "It isn't going to happen!" I say. "I'm tired of having no privacy. Thank you, but NO!"

How many people have watched me put my pants on these past weeks? My caregivers have become used to my aim for independence. They did what was necessary when it *was* necessary and are glad they have been relieved of some of the task. How many times has a pan of water and a towel been plunked down in front of me and for how many days, weeks even, has it been left up to me to wash and dress?

Have I not been unfailingly polite when my normally modest self has been viewed in sundry moments that all my life have been understood to be private?

On the toilet. At the sink as I wield a toothbrush. As I dip washcloth into water and clean myself.

Yesterday, when I was finally offered a shower, I refused because I'm no longer willing to rely on someone else or give away any of my personal dignity.

"No! No!" I repeat again and the ambitious therapist finally goes away. Later, she says my refusal meant she couldn't check off one of the goals set for me —to balance correctly while doing my morning tasks.

After days and days, they want to check my balance? *Now*?

Five more full days to go. This, too, shall pass.

No more coffee that tastes like warm water that had a coffee bean dragged through it.

No more cold mounds of pseudo scrambled eggs.

No more flabby white bread.

No more "genuine orange juice" that tastes

suspiciously like the canned dreck that I gave my children years ago, believing advertising that proclaimed its nutritive values.

Artificial food! Just as I know that now, they must have known it all along. (Whoever "they" are.) And this artificial food came to rest on the trays of rehab centers and will likely continue to do so unless, at some future time, there is a drastic change in the philosophy of care centers.

October 23

Clinton and Trump and all their players will campaign today. How can anyone stand this pace? I'm weary of it, even though I've hardly left my rehab room. How can all the people who have actual tasks to perform for these candidates continue to perform?

How many states will go for Trump in the election?

And soon we will be reviewing the definition of "electoral college" just as we do every four years. Hopefully, Clinton's win will be sufficiently large to make the discussion rhetorical.

A long, long Sunday ahead—my last in the Willows. Then, three more full days, one of them cut shorter by a medical appointment. And finally, home on Friday.

I've never taken my bills casually and am itching to be back at my desk so I can ascertain what entity has paid for what during this broken hip episode. This will be an interesting test. I pay for a lot of insurance over and above the automatic Medicare deduction

A Broken Hip Episode

from my Social Security checks and am, fortunately, so blessed with good health that there's been little need to collect.

So now that I've actually had surgery and been in the hospital and spent weeks in a rehab center, the final truth will out. Will I get a cascade of bills for all these services or will there be little cost left over to pay, or will there be any charges at all?

Hmmm.

October 24

Only four more nights to go!

No more 3:30 a.m. blood draws, no more 5:30 a.m. administration of a pill that can be taken at any time of day.

A new one last night: a CNA I didn't recognize came in at 2:30 or thereabouts, waking me.

"I don't need anything," I said.

"I'll just check!" she says.

Damned if she didn't head for the bed. This woman was going to check under my covers to see if I were wet!

Well, no.

"I get up and go to the bathroom by myself," I plead.

She stops, looks at me, and begins jumping up and down and clapping her hands like a game show participant.

I acknowledge the applause with as much graciousness as it's possible to muster at that hour of the night.

Such approbation for just peeing independently!

For sure, I am experiencing second childhood, hers if not mine.

A Broken Hip Episode

During therapy sessions, I'm now encouraged to put weight on my entire left foot. My tippy toe constraint is past!

The therapist bids me to stand up from my wheelchair, take up my walker and—*walk*. On both feet. The leg attached to my injured hip feels as if it's several inches longer than the other leg. Or is it shorter? This long-awaited use of both feet feels strange.

I hobble tentatively across the floor, followed by an aide with the wheelchair, walk until I'm tired and then sit down. Will there be pain later?

I've been sitting in a wheelchair up to twelve hours a day. Most days, at least ten hours with only therapy and short bathroom breaks to relieve the weariness.

Weekends, when there was little or no therapy, my time in the wheelchair often increased. How did I sleep after so much inactivity? But sleep I usually did, grateful for the relative comfort of lying down.

I think more about the cardiac diet: I don't know why it happened or why I didn't protest strenuously. Hard to eat with no seasoning but I recognize the motivation behind the doctor's orders—to help me reach a ripe old age despite broken bones.

But I hit a ripe old age several years ago.

I have never succumbed to this cardiac diet. I've just stopped eating as a solution and sent my trays back untouched. Nobody has ever commented on this, even though I believe it's generally understood that one's wellbeing depends upon good food. How does going without eating contribute to one's longevity? Is it a policy that inquiry should not be made lest the answer cause problems?

Tom Hayden has died, it says on television. The headlines of yore—yore being the late 1960s—when he stood up against the Vietnam war and then had the audacity to marry Jane Fonda. Or she had the audacity to marry him. The curses of society rained down upon them both.

But somewhere along in there, it became decent to stand up and protest things, political and social. I hope there is more and more of it in the future.

"CLINTON LEADS TRUMP BY ONE POINT IN NORTH CAROLINA!" That's not much but it's something.

Sometimes I am a little fearful when I am confronted with the idea that Trump can be even moderately successful in this contest. After all, there were plenty of people who voted against Obama's second term, even though they desperately needed "Obamacare" for their children. People who couldn't overcome their personal addictions; people who, in my estimation, were guilty of early and ignorant child abuse.

Is Trump doing well with these child abusers?

October 24

Today and tomorrow are the last usual days. Thursday is "get ready to go" day and also includes a medical appointment. Friday is GO! How now? It's very important to avoid accidents of all kinds and I find myself moving gingerly. I must stay off the floor and upright so my dismissal will be on schedule. A fear of falling has infiltrated my brain and may never go away.

Everyone is out on the campaign trail. The Clintons, the Obamas. Everyone in the world with a shred of credence is out fighting. People *without* a shred of credence are out fighting, too.

What might Trump be up to today? Fourteen days until the election.

He says, "We're winning!"

You know who's winning? The media! Bejillions spent on campaign advertising. What if that were spent on childhood poverty?

And to make sure everything is normal, another headline says, "Two shot in Virginia." It's like Groundhog Day. Everything happens over and over again.

A Broken Hip Episode

Trump says, "I know more about ISIS than the generals!"

This man is a dangerous egomaniac but he has a following, it seems. How will they handle a loss? He has said out loud the kind of thing that is usually concealed.

October 26

This is the next-to-last full day. Am I anxious?

Oh yes.

The *barely* tolerable of last week has this week become the intolerable.

Last night, for only the second time of my stay at the Willows, I asked for an anti-anxiety pill. It was 11:30, when I'd finally recognized the merry-go-round in my head and thought to ask for intervention. As always, Beard is prompt and pleasant. I vow not to get up in the night to go to the bathroom, for it is all too possible that the pill might make me too groggy to safely walk the distance.

Not to worry. I sleep from 11:40 to 7:00 and awaken dry as a bone.

CNN is skittering on. Rudy Giuliani is pontificating to a reporter. Who cares what he thinks? However, every pundit on earth has found a way to weigh in on the Trump thing.

A Canadian nurse is charged with killing eight

assisted living patients where she works. Can't have that, of course. Still, I wonder if the patients she murdered were sad people huddled in their beds/wheelchairs as they were forced to breathe and stay alive through intravenous intervention. And how many like them die each year from deliberate neglect? How many die because their families and doctors decide against this or that? The numbers escalate.

This is a terrible thing to be thinking about but I examine my innermost wishes and make a silent vow to get some things straight with my family.

One last time, I have my hair washed and combed. The young woman who does the hair in the Willows salon is good. Her own hair is decidedly a black do, today with red dye over the black and multiple braids, but she isn't limited. From week to week, I've watched her do a variety of hair and do it all well. There was a Caucasian man who looked as bedraggled and frowsy as I've looked myself much of my time here. He's in a wheelchair and has probably been here as long as me. The beautician goes at him delicately with a scissor, snipping here and there. When she has finished, this scraggly man has a professional haircut and looks like the business man he probably is, not a refugee from a sick room. I've seen ladies come in, their thin short hair in a dejected straggle and leave with fine white hair arranged as becomingly as any Federated Woman's Club might endorse.

I guess the moral is that if you're in one of these places you should get your hair done regularly. Compared to other things, it isn't very expensive.

Back from the beauty shop, the door to my room is wide open and the room is empty. It has been washed and waxed and is awaiting—not me, but the person who, in two days' time, will replace me.

I stay in the hall and wait patiently. To enquiring people who pass by, I declare myself homeless. It's a joke but I feel a little that way as well. Ejected; thrust out into a cold world by people who can't wait to see me gone.

Then, the floor is dry and they put the furniture and me back in our customary locations.

OCTOBER 27

My last day. My last night.

Home tomorrow and then the challenges will be self-imposed, except for whatever the home health person urges.

The therapists call me in and efficiently document whatever successes or semi-successes they think I've achieved.

One by one, the nursing assistants and others I've gotten to know come into my room at the end of their shifts and tell me goodbye. So nice of them to do that, and there are some who graciously make me feel as if they and I have crossed over, just a bit, into friendship. I pray that I've not made their lives difficult by making demands or whining or complaining. They have hard jobs and modest rewards.

The nurse comes in with numerous blister packages of pills—every kind that has been prescribed for me over the last few weeks: various kinds of opioids and anxiety meds, as well as the thyroid pills and blood thinners that I have been prescribed for years. Some of the packs, including the anxiety meds and most of the heavy-duty pain relievers, have only one or two pills missing since I've used Tylenol when possible.

"These are yours," she says.

"What do I need them for?" I ask.

"You paid for them, so they're yours," is the answer. "Just sign here that you've received them."

Bemused, I stick the packs into my already-packed bags. I'll give this situation some thought next week. Something about it makes me uneasy.

This afternoon my wheelchair is going to be removed and I'm dubious. At home, there will be alternative chairs to sit in, including the easy chairs where I've long loved to sit and watch the many birds collect at my feeders. But for the rest of this day I must sit in a straight-backed dining room chair after the wheelchair has been trundled away. That's dreadfully uncomfortable. A few weeks ago I was told that I'm entitled to an easy chair in my room but it never materialized and I didn't pursue getting one. Why is it essential for them to remove my wheelchair before I've gone my way? Surely, they have quite a few others on the premises that can be used if there's a need. Sometimes, it just seems as if common sense got waylaid someplace when the routines were devised.

A Broken Hip Episode

To the orthopedist this morning. It's a van ride away and the city I see, going and coming, is busy. At the medical center, I am x-rayed once again and told by the surgeon who operated on my hip that my break has healed. He doesn't do any elaborating and I'm told to come back in November. I decide to play nice and, in all sincerity, thank him for his skill on my behalf. For some reason, he looks surprised and his parting handshake is semi-cordial.

Amen. Amazing grace for an old lady stupid enough to step backward from a stool into thin air.

October 28

And so the day dawns.
    I'll go home and be happy to do so.
    Our house. Our garden. Our birds.

Nevertheless, I'll be leaving behind the nice people I've met here, more than a few, and I'll remember them for the rest of my life.
    I know from talking with them that many have dreams and plans and roads they want to travel. May it be so.
    Blessings on them all.
    The Trump saga that I've watched from my wheelchair and my bed won't end until eleven days from now. Being the terror he is, it probably won't end then but go on and on as long as the man can get attention.
    Pence's plane slid off the runway at LaGuardia. All ended well but if he had been hurt, Trump would have blamed in all on Hillary Clinton.
    This is assuming that she will win the election—our first woman president! What a marvelous thing that will be. By Inauguration Day in January, I should

A Broken Hip Episode

be walking without a walker, maybe driving.

If—oh no—but IF Trump should happen to win, my horror will be outsize and I'll have to count any remaining blessings very carefully.

I'm watching the clock. Patty will be here soon, with the walker that she has ordered.

"L'chaim," as my Jewish in-laws would say. To life!

Dene Hellman

Wong-Baker FACES Pain Rating Scale

| 0 | 2 | 4 | 6 | 8 | 10 |
| NO HURT | HURTS LITTLE BIT | HURTS LITTLE MORE | HURTS EVEN MORE | HURTS WHOLE LOT | HURTS WORST |

From Wong D.L., Hockenberry-Eaton M., Wilson D., Winkelstein M.L., Schwartz P.: *Wong's Essentials of Pediatric Nursing*, ed. 6, St. Louis, 2001, p. 1301. Copyrighted by Mosby, Inc. Reprinted by permission.

A Broken Hip Episode

At Home

November and December

"Mom, I'm scared!"

It's Jean, my youngest daughter, calling from Madison, Wisconsin.

Its 10:00 at night on November 8th and the election returns are coming in. Jean is seeing something astounding: Wisconsin, a state that frequently has voted for Democrats in recent years, is sliding into Republican terrain.

"Don't worry," I tell her. "Midwesterners are practical people. There's no way they could fail to recognize that Trump isn't up to being President!" We say goodnight but she doesn't sound very cheered.

We've been checking the available returns all evening and it isn't looking good in North Carolina, either. But then, from my viewpoint, elections often don't look good in this state and I didn't expect anything much to my liking. However, the reportage is broadening well beyond the borders of southern states and I feel physically and mentally unable to deal with it.

"I'm going to bed," I tell Patty.

A Broken Hip Episode

The next morning, I'm up before Patty leaves for her teaching job. As I hobble down the hall, maneuvering my walker toward the kitchen, I see her standing quietly in the middle of the room. She sees me coming; I look at her with a question on my face; she sadly shakes her head.

It's said that everyone who was alive at the time remembers where they were when they heard that President John Kennedy had been killed. I'm so old that I even remember where I was when my mother told me that President Franklin Roosevelt had died. There are a lot of people who will remember, in the coming years and decades, the moment when they heard that Donald Trump had been elected President.

Halloween had been great. It wouldn't have been practical for me to cope with handing out treats to the kids who rang our doorbell while, at the same time, clutching my walker, but it was fun seeing them through the living room window as grandson Phillip did the honors.

Pat and I began talking about Thanksgiving and Christmas coming up and I was distressed that, for the first time in memory, cooking would be beyond me and others would be left with all the chores.

And here I had been daydreaming for weeks about

what I'd be able to accomplish, physically, before the end of the year.

And now this wretched person in whom I had no shred of confidence had gone and gotten himself elected President of the United States!

"No depression allowed," warned I to me.

There was a new and regular visitor to our house, a physical therapist named Maria who was going to help me continue rehabilitation. She had records of what I'd done at the Willows, pages and pages of exercise diagrams that I should follow, both under her tutelage and by myself, plus a both-feet-on-the-ground air of expectation. She also had an agreeable smile and an accent that was quite easily understood. I hadn't known anybody else from the Philippines but I've since read that medical people are a major export from that country.

We got off to a good start. I had bird feeders; she said that she had bird feeders. From what she said, I deduced that she lived in an exceptionally nice house that she shared with a couple of other therapists.

So, I thought, this therapy work pays well and she is well-settled in to local life. Good. The day after the election, she commiserated with me over my unhappiness at Trump's political success and said

A Broken Hip Episode

that she was a little bit tired of hearing so many of her clients say bigoted things that indicated they had voted for him.

"From what I read," I said, "you have a controversial new president in the Philippines, too."

Rodrigo Duterte, at seventy-one the oldest person to ever be elected President in the Phillipines, had been in office since the last of May, 2016, and was causing international consternation over his advocated method of handling criminals. He claimed to have personally done away with a few of the 1400 who had already been dispatched. He subsequently became expansive and advocated killing tens of thousands more.

He bested three or four rivals for the presidency, gaining almost 40% of the votes as Philippine citizens ushered him into office.

"He's really something!" I said to Maria. "At least, Trump hasn't so far advocated punishment without a trial. This Duterte is one scary dude."

"I voted for him," she said.

Maria meant business and we didn't waste time. We marched up and down the bedroom hall, with and without the walker. I was terrified, despite assurance that she was right beside me, prepared to buffer any unsteadiness. The hundreds of calisthenics that she directed me to do on the safety of my bed and the ones I did while I sat in a chair were designed to make me strong and limber. I wasn't particularly impressed with their potential and longed for more spectacular procedures.

But they probably did work, although improvement wasn't dramatic. In the evenings, Patty often encouraged me to walk without an aid but I had to be coaxed and wouldn't have done it without her beside me, doling out copious amounts of encouragement and reassurance.

This hesitance would never leave me and, regrettably, I doubt that it ever leaves anyone who has experienced a bad fall with an accompanying shattering of bone. I've heard plenty of stories about people who have allowed the fear of falling to affect them so much that, forever after, they have to be wheeled where they need to go. Did I want to be one of *them?* No, but I certainly understood them.

So I toddled up and down the house using whatever props I needed, did thousands of boring exercises, and pumped my legs up and down maniacally when nobody was looking. But if I were on my feet, alone, and in real need to get from point A to point B, bedroom to bathroom to kitchen, I clung

A Broken Hip Episode

with sweaty palms to the handle of my walker.

Maria and I set a goal. Actually, it probably was *her* goal and she persuaded me of its importance. By the time she and I were scheduled to part company, sometime before the first of the new year, I was supposed to be walking with a cane, my walker retired to the garage.

Gulp. Annie, my Iowa daughter, got into the act at that point and sent me a beautiful cane. Being Annie, who always goes the second mile, she actually sent me *two* canes, a black one and a red one. We named the black one "Matthew" and the red one "Scarlett." I decided that Matthew would be the cane that I learned on and Scarlett would stay in my car to be used when I was out in public.

In the meanwhile, Maria and I struggled with my self-confidence. "I am here," she said—over and over—as I shuffled up and down the bedroom hall, terrified that I'd slip or that my legs would fold up under me.

The summer before my fall, I had gone shoe shopping in a place that specialized in good sport shoes. My feet were as old as the rest of me and probably in even worse shape so it took effort to keep them relatively comfortable. Years before, I'd had bunion surgery on a foot that was so painful that, wherever I was, I took my shoes off: at home, in church, in movie theaters, in restaurants. As soon as I got settled, off would come the shoes. Sometimes they navigated quite some distance away and I or my companion of the hour would have to make an embarrassed search.

A friend recommended a chiropodist and I went through a painful bunionectomy. After the operated foot healed, I said to him, "Now, what about the other foot?" He looked at it, perhaps saw potential tribulations that he didn't want to deal with, and said, "It's not going to be a problem."

What he didn't reckon with, maybe, was that I was going to go on living for years, even decades, more. That eventually that "other" foot would end up skewed in a strange direction and have a couple of hammer toes. It definitely *was* going to be a problem. At some point, I should have consulted an orthopedist but I was enjoying my release from painful bunions so I let it go. Big mistake.

As time went on, shoes were still part of my vanity. My feet, especially the one that hadn't been attended to, aged faster than the rest of me so I tried to find acceptable and inconspicuous styles.

A Broken Hip Episode

All of which led to my summer visit to a store that specialized in good sport shoes. I was down to thinking that I'd have to live much of my life in stout, traditional tennis shoes that would dictate final years of always looking like a has-been athlete. The store was pretty much self-serve and I tried on a range of athletic shoes, a bunch of moccasins, and just about every other pair that looked as if it were designed for all-day wear. I hung on to one pair of unassuming little blue mesh shoes until the last and when I finally did put them on I knew it for a "eureka" moment. The shoe box said they were Sketcher Go Walks. They cost as much as the more sturdy-looking tennis shoes but anything that felt that good was worth it.

I wore them out of the store. I wore them all day, every day; fortunately, they were up to periodic sloshing in the laundry while holding their shape and size. I had them on when I climbed up on the itty-bitty stool to hang curtains and flew backward to the floor. I had them on when I was transferred from the hospital to the Willows. I wore them every day in the Willows and suspected they were getting pretty ripe.

When I got home from rehab, the little blue mesh shoes continued to do full service on each and every day. Last things off at night, first things on in the morning.

There was still some pain in my hip but I was determined to take nothing but Tylenol if I needed relief. The packets of "leftover" pills that had been pressed upon me when I left the Willows simmered in my dresser drawer. Some of them promised longer sleep at night but I had reservations about them and was not seduced. Then, as the first days and weeks slipped away, my reservations grew and I finally realized that I didn't want to use them at all.

Disposal was a pain. Each pill was in its own little blister pack so each had to be carefully punched out to be discarded. I'd heard that one did not flush prescription drugs down the toilet or wash them away in the sink. Ultimately, I crushed each pill and mixed it with used coffee grounds that were destined for the garbage. It was a long, messy process, involving a mere six to eight pills a day and there were probably better ways to go. But if it involved turning them in to someone, somewhere, I didn't have any confidence in that method, either. Although I've never had any interest in using much alcohol or other substances that could alter my state of mind, I knew that some people aren't that fortunate. It just wouldn't seem right to put the pills in the hands of someone who might possibly be susceptible to their misuse and no information about alternative disposal was available.

As the pills became one with soggy coffee grounds, I tore up the renewal prescriptions that came with them and was thankful when the entire situation was finally over and done with.

Patty had a few days off at Thanksgiving and at Christmas and my appreciation of her company allayed the depressive tendencies that were agitating away in the back of my mind. We had time to share mutual despair over Trump's election and discuss whatever else was happening in the world. We happily followed my grandson Patrick's bicycle tour of Israel on Facebook. When Maria told me that her therapy time with me was over. I took her picture in front of the Christmas tree and vowed to go on exercising.

When she rang the doorbell on the last day, I triumphantly opened the door minus my walker and with cane in hand.

January and February

One of the hardest things that I faced was that I couldn't do much—and that went beyond not being able to do any cooking or assisting with house upkeep. I couldn't do much for myself and the lack of personal independence was appalling. I have a stubborn need for autonomy as, I think, do most people.

With never an impatient or irritable look, Patty gave me showers, washed my hair and my clothes, made my meals and laid them out when she couldn't be home, kept my room tidy, kept track of my medical appointments and made arrangements so I could keep them. She changed my sheets, and emptied the contents of the commode that kept me from having to make long treks down the hall to the bathroom during late night hours.

I was resolved that it was going to stop; the first thing I took on was doing my own baths and shampoos. Patty's room had a walk-in shower so it was practical to use that at the beginning.

"How would you like a shower and a shampoo tonight?" she'd say when she got home from school.

A Broken Hip Episode

I was always more than ready for it, although there was something about stripping down, then stepping into the shower to be attended to—just as I'd done for my kids when they were young—that left me feeling not so much embarrassed for my nudity as self-conscious about the bumps and sags that go with aging.

"I wish I knew what to do about the way my belly sags," I'd say, remembering the days when my daughters and I were all younger and they had been proud of the way I looked in a swim suit when we went to the beach.

Pat would graciously demur, insisting that I had no such sags, and was tactful about holding up my bathrobe so I could scramble into it as soon as possible.

The bathroom I'd used before the hip break had a typical shower/tub setup. When we'd updated the room, we were told that the tub was solid cast iron that would require a fortune to remove, should we fancy a walk-in shower. Reluctantly, we commissioned a facelift for the tub and let it go.

No problem at the time but now it was. How on earth could I ever step over the side of the tub to use the shower? It did have a safety device that we'd clamped on a couple of years before, so that was something. Still, there was that sixteen-inch tub wall that had to be clambered over, bad hip and all.

I began to practice, when nobody was around. Hanging on to the safety handle, shod in my blue mesh shoes and wearing the fleece sweat pants and tops that I'd inaugurated in the Willows and continued to wear after I got home, I would brace myself and then step into the tub. And step out again. And step in again. And step out again until I had it down to the point where I could do it in an upright position instead of a kind of doubled up crouch. One morning when I was alone in the house I undressed, made sure a towel and bath mat were handy and took a shower.

When Patty got home and said, "Would you like a shower?" it was satisfying to say—ever so casually—"Oh, I used the one in my bathroom today."

I could tell that she was struggling to keep her thoughts to herself and her facial expression free of anxiety as she nodded and said, "Okay."

My next crusade was to change the sheets on my bed. I wasn't a rowdy sleeper so from the start I could pull up the covers on my bed, plump the pillows, and smooth the bedspread. I'd already been doing that in the Willows. But *changing* sheets, now that was something else. I can recall when fitted sheets were one of the newest inventions in the world of housekeeping. They solved a problem that was as old as modern civilization—how to restore a sleeping place to a tidy appearance in an efficient amount of time. My mother had simply taken all of the bed linens off the bed each morning, piled them all in a chair, and then put them back on, tidying, smoothing, tucking as she went, and coaching me in how to do the same with my own bed.

Fitted sheets corrected all that and soon sheets were being sold in colors other than white and were sometimes glorified with designs. However, if the sheets were going to adhere to the bed during the night they had to be quite snug. The end consequence was that, depending upon the generosity of the sheet dimensions and/or the heft of the mattress, those fitted sheets could be a hellish struggle. Some tore; some were so skimpy that they never did encompass the mattress corners; some were tidy and snug on three corners and the fourth corner would end up half-covered. This was par whether they were inexpensive or high-grade.

Then, of course, the blanket that covered the top sheet had to be the right dimension so it could be drawn up close at night and be discreet about how far it hung on the other three sides. Would it tuck in at the foot without causing too much muscle power? Would it droop down lower than the bedspread when the bed was fully made?

Another effort before all was right: the bedspread had to be coped with. There again, a bit of a struggle. Could it be folded back gracefully, with just enough fabric to be practical? Was it long enough on the sides to cover the blanket when the bed was made?

An appropriate Monday morning arrived. A fresh set of sheets and pillowcases in hand, I approached the bed, and somehow got the bedspread, blanket, and top sheet pulled off. Good! This was half the battle.

But no, it wasn't. The fitted sheet had to be worked with, corner by corner. Then the top sheet and the blanket each had to be labored over, smoothed, tucked. Then the pillowcases. Then the bedspread.

The job took me most of the morning, with a frequent time out to sit down, plot my next move, and force myself to get back at it.

Patty didn't take that one easily. I'd never heard her discuss fitted sheets but it seemed that she harbored hard feelings toward them and had developed techniques for managing them.

A Broken Hip Episode

"I can do that in no time at all!" she declared of the bed linen changing. "Just leave it for me after this!"

Nope.

With bath and linen changing milestones conquered, the next item on my list was doing my own laundry.

I love doing laundry. I always have. Not ironing so much, when ironing was a big undertaking that involved what my mother called *sprinkling* the items to be ironed, letting them mellow for an hour or so as they lay nicely rolled up in a basket meant for that purpose, then going at them with as hot an iron as the fabric allowed. And my mother thought everything needed ironing. Sheets. Nightgowns and pajamas. Pillowcases. Hand towels and dish towels. An assortment of shirts, blouses, dresses and pants relatable to every member of the household.

If wash day—always Monday—were a nice day, freshly washed items blew themselves smooth as they waved on a long outdoor clothes line. My mother sang on those days and I loved hearing her so happy.

If it were a nice day. That might have been twenty of fifty-two Mondays in a year. In the Midwest, where I grew up, the wind blew ferociously. Or it rained, causing a rush to the backyard to gather in nearly dry laundry before it got soaked. Or the temperature was cold enough to stiffen the hands that clamped on the clothes pins and then the items hanging on the line froze stiff, which necessitated carrying them inside to finish drying while draped over every chair and table that accommodated their presence.

By the time I was a young housewife with children, automatic washers and driers had come on the market. My husband was a teacher and we didn't have enough money to buy these marvelous machines when Patty and Annie were little, but by the time their younger sisters came along there was no such thing in the world of laundry as wringer washers. If one didn't have the money to buy one of the automatic devices there surely was one of the newfangled businesses called *laundromats* where one could take one's dirty clothes.

Did I say that I loved doing laundry? Maybe it was attributable to the wonder of finally owning one of these machines that washed things, then rinsed things, then spun them to a dampened stage wherein they could be transferred to another machine that would dry them.

A Broken Hip Episode

And there was this new process called "permanent press" which meant that lots of things didn't have to be ironed at all. Even sheets, fitted or otherwise.

I also know that part of my happiness with doing laundry can be traced to the part of me that is OCD. To the power of gathering up everything that had seen use in preceding days, including clothes worn by family members, towels used in the kitchen and bathroom, tablecloths—anything, really, that was fabric and could harbor a smudge or a germ. *And* to the hanging of freshly washed and ironed curtains that would be my downfall one September day in the future.

A day came in February when I sought to reassume my power over these smudges and germs. As long as my strength held out, I reasoned, I could make as many trips between my room and the washing machine as were required to get the job done. The problem was that we had an almost-new washing machine—an Asian model that we had chosen after much consumer research, sales-rep lauding and family discussion. It was expensive but, if it stopped working at some point, all one had to do was hold a telephone to its side and, presumably, someone with expertise would make it better from a distance.

In the place of a few dials to twist, it had buttons—many, many buttons that offered an encyclopedic range of options.

And it was tall. And I'm short. True, a starting button caused it to evenly position the laundry items, but when a load had finally been washed, it didn't transfer to the dryer. It could beep imperiously that it was finished but that was all. Short persons had to stand on tip-toe and lean over to reach newly washed items to then be placed in the dryer (which was old and had just a few dials.)

Standing on tiptoe and bending over isn't easy to do while hanging on to a walker or a cane but, eventually, I mastered the skill.

Behold! I could get in and out of a tub to wash myself, I could change my sheets, and I could do my laundry! There were a few other things that I needed to do for myself:

I wanted to drive my car.
I wanted to do my share of household chores.
I wanted to do my share of cooking.
I wanted to go shopping.

A Broken Hip Episode

On January 20, Donald Trump took the oath of office. I'd seen and heard other men take that oath over many decades. I didn't care for all of those men but usually reminded myself that ideas and motives change from time to time and that we probably would all manage until the next presidential election.

But I'd thought this was the election when, at last, we were going to see and hear a woman take the oath. I had dreamed about that for most of my life, never quite understanding why it didn't happen when so many other countries demonstrated the competence of woman leaders.

And now, here was this man whose agenda—or lack of one—represented ideas and motives that are an abhorrence to all the people whose opinions I respect. Not one single person of my acquaintance had voted for him or regarded him as worthy of deference. But someone—lots of someones—had to have so voted. Evidently, I had a limited acquaintance.

As a family of teachers, oaths of office by presidents had been made manifest to students, term after term. In my teaching years, in my mother's, in Patty's, in her paternal grandmother's, in the very long American history teaching career of Patty's father, it was considered a duty to put this illustration of America's sacred privilege before students.

As Patty went out the door to school on January 20, 2017, I said, "Are you going to tune in to the inauguration for your class?"

"I don't want to see it and I wouldn't wish it on anybody else," she said. I understood perfectly.

But people had voted this person into the presidency and I was well aware that, at my age, I'd likely not be around for another such ceremony so I turned on the television to watch and listen to this catastrophe that had happened to our country.

It was worse than I'd imagined. For an hour and a half, or thereabouts, Donald Trump read the speech that someone had written for him and that he must have endorsed, a speech that used the most negative words possible—*American carnage, rusted out factories peppered across the land like tombstones, trapped in poverty.* On and on it went and astute camera people often aimed at the past presidents who sat on the dais as proof that we are an orderly land that accepts changes in government leaders. The looks on the faces of these past presidents were grim as they heard from this lout, who could not put together an erudite remark of his own, opine that their administrations had done nothing except create carnage, rust and poverty.

A Broken Hip Episode

But there had to be people who voted for him. Who were they? This was the real question of the hour.

I began a search for information and at first there wasn't a lot out there. "It's the people in the Midwest," I heard. That opinion needed qualifying. I'd grown up in the Midwest and, later, often visited there, through the elections and administrations of seven Democrats and six Republicans—Trump making the seventh one of the Republicans. I don't know how Iowans voted in any of those elections but can't recall feeling overwhelmed the way I now was. My daughter, Annie, lives in Iowa and goes to many and many of the stump speeches by would-be candidates. She has plenty of funny anecdotes as well as descriptions of handshakes—whose was perfunctory and dry, whose offered a suggestion of good will.

Even though Hillary Clinton had won the popular vote, the archaic electoral college had put Donald Trump, with his lesser total of about sixty-three million votes, into the presidency.

However, sixty-three million is a lot of votes. *Whodunit?*

There were immediate speculations and

explanations that mostly pointed the finger at rural populations everywhere and people with little education. At white people, in general, especially men, who didn't want a woman president. At white women for whatever reason. Later, it was conceded that people who lived in cities had, in general, declined to vote for Trump but speculation was rife about which entities hadn't voted at all.

I wasn't very knowledgeable about regional political preferences even though, years before, I had moved from the Midwest to the Carolinas and in so doing had become acquainted with a lot of folks who came from New York and New Jersey as well as native Carolinians. Not one of these people was pro-Trump. But somehow or another, it seemed that I'd managed to live in ignorance of this country for eighty-seven years even as I'd congratulated myself on my well-rounded life.

Before long the book lists filled with tales of the several "nations" within the United States, as well as economic diversity that affects voters. I began to order and read them and, to some degree, information began supplanting gut fury. I still get in line for "hate Trump" exercises but, barring any sudden and terrible revelations, I'll hope that we keep up better with social and economic changes, as well as with population trends and do better in future elections.

Anguish about the election took up time, but I couldn't let it overwhelm. I had a book in the hopper that was scheduled for publication in the spring and I needed to park my behind, hip and all, into my office chair and do the last round of revisions and rewrites.

All to the good. When I face the screen and write, I'm lost to the world around me. This new book, *A House for Her*, was a collection of short-stories. Although I'd written poetry, essays, memoirs, and a novel, short-story writing was a skill I wanted to develop. For several years, maybe for a lifetime, I studied the stories of the best (Poe, O'Henry, de Maupassant, and on to Thurber, Shirley Jackson, Eudora Welty) in the hope of figuring out what made them work. In my youth, popular women's magazines published good short-stories instead of endless articles of soul-searching and both my mother and I read and discussed them.

Many books have been written on the subject of short-story writing skills. My father owned some now-archaic ones that he had tucked away in his motorcycle when he decided in the mid-1920s to cross the country from New York, following the Lincoln Highway to the west coast where he would settle down, write short-stories and illustrate them.

His journey ended halfway, when he met my mother and her family in Iowa, but the books were never thrown out and I found them in our home bookcase early on, when books first began attracting me. I read them when a teen and, while I recall no useful instructions, I wish I had them now. They probably were great. The one word I do recall was *hackneyed.* Authors were urged to avoid writing *hackneyed* material and I didn't know what that meant.

Anyway, getting a book ready for current publication was terrific medicine for my dual predicament of hip break problems and Trump's election triumph. If either body or soul were in pain while I replotted and rephrased, my brain was too lost in my computer to take note of it. I hope none of what I wrote was hackneyed.

By the end of February, I was ready to give up my cane when at home and get around the house without it. There was no sense of increased safety connected with this nor any grace to my movement. Daughter Ann had contracted with a security service and insisted that I wear a tag around my neck at all times that required a mere push from me to bring ambulances and other emergency vehicles careening into our street. I hated it but wore it faithfully while begging her at intervals to terminate the service.

One leg had turned out to be shorter than the other, which caused me to hobble and there were no techniques to overcome that, although wearing a Dr. Scholl's insert in one shoe helped. Practicing my balance, something I'd have to do for the rest of my life, was iffy. I took up wall and furniture surfing as if by instinct.

It's hard to explain what is so reassuring and steadying about putting one hand, lightly, on a stretch of wall or piece of furniture as one moves from place to place. I hope that whatever wit gave it the "surfing" name, was doing it personally, not as a sarcastic "other" who was looking on. Jokes are made, I know, but if you don't need to wall surf, don't knock it. Those of us who are experiencing walking as a relearned accomplishment need all the help we can get.

March and April

One of the wonders of the middle South is the long spring and long autumn. To a native Iowan, grown to adulthood amid snow drifts and tentative spring seasons that quickly slide into hot summers, I was especially happy about the arrival of March. Patty had enthusiastically taken up gardening in recent years and she was now engrossed in the creation of a big perennial plot. It would eliminate much of the hard-to-mow sloping lawn in front of our house and provide the basis for what the two of us considered fascinating conversations about its progress.

So there was that and my concentration on my hip began to go away. Even though I couldn't do any digging and weeding, the spring sunshine was glorious and I took to sitting outside for a time each morning, sans sun block, to soak it up. A lot of the rays applied directly to my psyche; I turned eighty-eight early in April and needed the encouragement.

Still, sitting in the sunshine and admiring gardens left gaps. My reliable though ancient car, my '99 Honda CRV, sat in the driveway, driven now and then to keep it in good health, but a constant reminder that it had been idle for six months—which wasn't good for it. And, in some ways, so had I and it wasn't good for me either.

Similar to my efforts to get in and out of my bathtub, I started doing that with the Honda. Fortified with a cane and my trusty blue mesh shoes, I'd open the door on the driver side and try to get in. Our long sloping driveway made it harder than it would have been had the car been on level ground but, eventually, I worked out a system wherein I'd back up to the seat and heave my behind onto its edge, then squirm until I was in place. The CRV seats sit high, a feature that I'd always appreciated, but maybe not so much at present.

It took days, maybe three weeks of practicing, before I could confidently situate myself behind the steering wheel with both feet properly located in front of me and my cane in a position where I could easily grasp it when I got to wherever I was going.

And where was it that I meant to go? That wasn't something to ponder for long because two reasons for being able to drive shortly presented themselves. One, Annie was going to visit us and when Annie visited we delighted in going places. Two, a client needed to get a new project underway and that required some mobility on my part. In addition to writing my own material, I do some writing and editing projects for companies, organizations and individuals. That part of my life had been on hold during the past months and I missed the stimulation.

Once able to get myself into the driver's seat, I began driving around the block so I wouldn't be scared of piloting a moving vehicle. One of my early destinations was to a regimen of physical therapy sessions prescribed by my doctor. They were okay but didn't add much to my walking abilities. Each was supervised by a different therapist from the one I'd last seen, working from notes left in a log book by the previous therapist. A few of them were fantastic and I regretted that I'd never see them again. A few seemed to be still in training. I'm glad that I decided to end the sessions fairly soon because I then discovered that my insurance had run out and the cost for the private therapy sessions had been steep. In a perfect world, therapy would go on as long as it is needed, but I'd been fortunate to have had access to as much as I had.

There was no longer an excuse for staying away from former activities, whether a book club or Sunday morning services. Being self-conscious

A Broken Hip Episode

because I now hobbled was distorted vanity. There was, of course, the realization that my blue mesh shoes weren't cut out for such refined activities and the search for their fellow shoes began. It got to be a bit expensive when I turned up a modest variety of Sketchers online and in a few shoe stores and wanted one pair of each. Other shoe manufacturers were beginning to display similar styles, but I wasn't yet ready to experiment so my shoe shelves began to fill with a variety of colors and limited variations of the blue ones. Elegant pumps goodbye—probably forever.

Annie's visit was, as always, a joy. She has a way of bringing excitement with her and it's always fun to think up places to go and things to do that will allow her a change from her busy life of work and the care of the many cats and dogs that she has adopted in her years as an animal rescuer.

Knowing that my stamina was now limited, she was also thinking of things we could do that we'd all enjoy without a great output of energy and time. When she came up with, "Let's all go and have a manicure!" it did seem extravagant to Patty and me even though Annie insisted it was her treat.

Between the two of us, we had likely not had more than three or four manicures –tending toward such an indulgence only when somebody was getting married. We had learned, through a sort of osmosis, that nail salons now proliferated but we hadn't gone so far as to notice in what locations they were.

Annie settled that information gap by getting on the phone and online to do research so, before long, we were filing into a salon within blocks of our house and ordering some mysterious thing called "French tips." It took quite a while before all three of us were finished and ready to go out to dinner and, once seated with menu in hand, I continuously peeked at my hands and couldn't believe what I saw. Later, and for the time the manicure lasted, the sight of my rare impeccable nails continued to amaze. How could I have lived my entire life without them?

When the manicure finally began wearing off, I went back to the salon and got another. And another after that. It was probably late August before I was willing to forego manicures. While they were still in process, I realized that after my broken hip episode I had become nonchalant about my grooming and that I persisted in dragging around in the sagging knit pants and tops I'd worn in the Willows while my other clothes hung unused in the closet.

Hobbling and the use of canes, I lectured myself, don't make any kind of excuse for letting oneself give up on grooming. Nobody has to go that route since jeans and tee shirts are a national costume, available in all levels of financial outlay that are mostly indistinguishable from one another. As for professional manicures—they're nice to have but, during the years when I wasn't looking, more long-lasting polishes suitable for home use have come on the market.

Such complacencies aside, something bad *was* happening, probably *had* been happening for some time and I'd ignored it. I was losing hair. It was no longer possible to ignore it; it began to litter the bathroom floor. Since I was not yet doing any of the sweeping, dusting and dry mopping that are part of routine house care, it had been possible to avoid the entire scenario. Patty might have noticed but hadn't said anything.

Losing hair is a normal part of things. It happens to everyone, at times, and then the loss stops and we forget all about it until the next time. This wasn't like that. There was more and more hair falling out and it didn't stop. The part was widening, the comb that I routinely ran through my hairbrush yielded excess hair every day and it occurred to me that I might soon be partly bald. Still, I was reluctant to talk about it or do any research. I'd faced all kinds of stuff in the past few months, overcome some things and resigned myself to others. Why take on another problem?

But time was up for looking the other way; I'd do the damn research I said to myself and began looking in medical literature and asking questions online. It didn't take long to turn up a logical cause for my hair loss.

Stress, said the medical gurus. A good hard injury to the body, in particular. What would a person expect who had been through injury, surgery and long term recovery? And it *would* eventually stop and the hair *would* grow again.

It was reassuring but a little disconcerting, too, because I now realized that my ego had been running more of the show than I cared to confront. A stiff upper lip is one thing but underneath all the faked serenity that person inside—the one that hunkers down with the shades drawn—knows perfectly well when stress is present and tries to look the other way.

At the end of April, seven and a half months after the broken hip episode, I was ready to move on from the recovery process and, with newfound objectivity, began exploring other areas of my psyche.

The review turned up some hidden surprises. Upstaged by the efforts to regain physical and mental

A Broken Hip Episode

stability, as well as my dismay at Trump's election, I hadn't explored some of the negatives, including anger, connected with my six weeks in rehab.

I still thought that the Willows' staff had been great and much deserving of praise and appreciation. The resentment that I harbored was entirely due to realization that the rehab's ownership was conspicuously dedicated to profit. They were spending money on improvements in physical layout but the food was bad, the staff had too few professionals and those were kept busy handing out meds. There was a doctor who made patient visits but spoke with an accent so heavy that elderly people with limited ability to distinguish sounds couldn't understand her. Probably, she reflected more savings. Nobody ever made an effort to find out what patients might find problematic or puzzling about their daily lives. Problems like: a) Why aren't you eating? b) Have you had a shower or shampoo (or some other personal need) that has been overlooked? c) Do you have a personal worry that we aren't aware of?

Simply put, the rigid protocol had no room for discoveries that might cost money. Discoveries that a fresh green salad was a rarity and a half-banana once in a while didn't fulfill a need for fresh fruit. That vegetables straight out of a can, never seasoned much or alternated with fresh ones, were less than appetite-inducing. That the price paid for a day in the rehab bore no relationship to the services received. That unappetizing food, day after day, induces depression.

One of the reasons for my after-the-fact concern was due to Paul and Marcia, who took me out to lunch one day. We had a good time over Mexican fare in a restaurant located not far from my house and were careful to keep the outing short so I wouldn't run out of strength. Paul is a retired physician and said when he helped me to the door, "Do you know how lucky you are? Many people your age can't go home again after a hip break. Half of them die."

No, I had no idea. Why would that be? My broken hip had caused a lot of pain and, to some extent, had changed my life—but not come home? Or die? Those alternatives were terrible. As I pondered during the next weeks, reviewed my own experiences, investigated statistics online and asked friends and relatives about cases they might have encountered, considerable information fell into place and made me want to explore more thoroughly.

A Broken Hip Episode

May and June

May is a great month, almost everywhere. My three daughters who live in the upper Midwest get a break from the weather and it's certainly glorious in North Carolina.

I was often in and out of the garden, loving this respite before the summer heat was due to set in, thrilling to the flowers that came and went in luxurious displays. My own gardening was limited to replanting the window box in the courtyard but I'd discovered ivy geraniums the year before and, now that I could again drive, found delight in hunting for new colors. Even that little bit of getting my hands into the soil was a satisfaction.

The new book of short-stories was well received and a greater satisfaction than I'd expected. Most of the stories had Midwestern settings and people "up there" who read them particularly liked them. "Why the Midwest?" was sometimes asked and I explained that viewing a setting in absentia allows for a broader perspective. After all, there had been a time when fashionable writers had poked about Europe while writing of life in the United States.

Not ready to begin writing another book until autumn and occupied with projects for clients, I used extra time to pursue my interest in defining the social and/or intellectual imbalances that had led to the election of Trump to the presidency.

Beginning with a hypothesis that I'd encountered since the election, that it was a "lower class" sort of voter, I went looking. With a good many things on my mind, an assortment of scholarly texts with extensive footnotes wasn't my preference but that turned out to be easily dealt with. A good many writers, it seemed, had already been observing and thinking, not about the likes of Trump but about the way our country's various paths had diverged. The books piled up on my bedside table and, with varying degrees of appreciation, I read *White Trash* (Nancy Isenberg, 2016) exploring the fallacy of there ever having been a classless society in 400 years of United States history; *Hillbilly Elegy* (J. D. Vance, 2016) about the disintegration of the poor white working class; *American Nations* (Colin Woodard, 2011) about regional cultures in the United States—and endless articles in current periodicals.

Fascinating as many of the writings were, since most preceded Trump's election I was still stumped about what had gone crazy in political thinking.

Somewhere, I did find an article that Michael Moore had published back in July 2016, four months before Trump won election and when the world in general was predicting a solid win for Hillary Clinton. It was entitled "Five Reasons Why Trump Will Win" and had been the cause for a good bit of denial and ridicule by critics. I read it with dropped jaw. Here is a synopsis of the reasons he gave:

1) Four states in the upper Great Lakes—Michigan, Ohio, Pennsylvania, and Wisconsin—that make up the United States rust belt had an embittered working class. The Clintons had supported NAFTA, and NAFTA had screwed the working class. Trump, they were told, would undo all that.

2) It was the last stand of the angry white man. A woman was about to take over! The male-dominated, 240 year run of the USA male was coming to an end. Can't have that!

3) Hillary is unpopular. The kids don't like her even though, thanks to Hillary and other women of her generation, these young millennial women won't ever be told to go bake some cookies instead of getting involved in government.

4) The average Bernie Sanders enthusiast is disappointed and, while she/he will probably vote for Hillary, they aren't going to evidence any enthusiasm. Who knows? They might even cast a vote for some off-the-main-course entity like the Green party candidate.

5) The Jesse Ventura Effect wherein mischievous voters don't like the choices and will vote for Trump just because it would be a practical joke and you can do anything you want in that voting booth and they won't find out so why not express your dark sense of humor like those Minnesota folks did a few years back when they voted in that wrestler?

The only thing that Moore wasn't predicting was interference by the Russians. I can't say that I now had a clear understanding of what went wrong but I at least had a fuzzy mental image. Putting together this and other things I'd read, Hillary Clinton was evidently defeated by evangelical working class white males who were chauvinistic practical jokers speaking with a Russian accent!
Or something like that.

It occurred to me that, going forward, it was time

A Broken Hip Episode

for mature women to call the shots. *All of our lives we have never figured in anybody's assessment of what has happened politically, worldwide, or what might happen in the future.* Moore had touched on the anger of men about the "rise" of women's importance in society but he certainly didn't suggest that this accelerated importance could change the vote in any way. This annoyed me but then I had a recollection. The first election that I was aware of was the one where Franklin Delano Roosevelt was running against Wendell Willkie. My mother, a lifelong Republican due to her family heritage, was enthused about Willkie and was mildly annoyed at the way my father leaned over the radio beaming with appreciation during an FDR speech. "Mah friends," FDR would intone, and my dad looked as if he definitely counted himself among the friends.

The day to vote arrived and my parents headed off to our village's town hall. I knew for certain that Dad would cast his vote for Roosevelt, so when they got home, I said to Mom, "So who did you vote for?"

I knew the answer in advance. She was a Wilkie person.

She almost snarled at me, "I voted for Roosevelt!"

Even at my young age, I thought that was peculiar. "Why?" I asked. "You like Wilkie better."

"Because," my mother said, "a woman should vote the way her husband does."

I was just a kid but that answer shocked me and never was erased from my brain. I thought about it more deeply as I grew older. Why had my mother been a Republican? Because her father had been! Why did she think she had to vote like him and later like her husband? Because that was the way women were trained to think and, with too few exceptions, that was the way it was. Always. Since time began. These days, most of the younger women know better but even too many of them are probably still listening quietly as the men in their lives expound.

Which leaves *us*—a horde of aging women, many of us no longer with a man in our lives whose expounding we are willing to listen to. We often are physically unable to get out to marches and other demonstrations, but we all can vote—by absentee ballot at the very least.

There are a lot of us because we tend to outlive everybody. The others have had their chance for eons and we sure as hell can do better! Vote. Talk. Write letters to your friends, your kids, the rest of your relatives. Some of them won't appreciate it but, at your age, you shouldn't worry about what they think is appropriate for you to say.

A Broken Hip Episode

July and August

Since Patty and I began sharing a household in June 2010, my favorite time of the year is from mid-June to mid-August because that's when teachers have a break and I love having Pat's company. Some teachers take temporary jobs to supplement iffy incomes, some go to school to enhance their educations, some are at a point in their lives when they can spend time on children, gardening, maybe a bit of travel. Pat had done all of those things in the past but this summer was going to include getting me steadier on my feet.

We would walk. Every day. Up and down the quiet street where we live. Regardless of the weather. It was a splendid idea and I liberated the rollater from its corner in the den. We had purchased it the previous October when collecting equipment for home use. It had wheels and a basket, handlebars and a fold down seat—all embellishments to make it a good travelling companion when out in public. I'd preferred getting around in public by using a walking stick, but when Pat and I set out to make daily hikes up and down the street we knew that it would take something with wheels to make it a tolerably pleasant experience.

We started out covering short distances that, over the weeks, lengthened. They were never very long, even though it took me quite a while to negotiate them. Pat must have been bored with the snail pace, but she entertained no excuses to skip the walk. I was often whiny, especially when the weather grew hotter and when that happened, Pat would suggest that we walk earlier, in the cool of the morning. After all, she knew all the grumbling techniques from her years as a teacher of adolescents.

And I did get incrementally stronger, which carried over to the times when I did other things that included shopping and running errands. Plus, it is always a luxury when a parent gets to have uninterrupted time for conversation with an adult child. When all was over, that's the part about those walks up and down the street that made it all such a pleasurable time.

(One of the things we often talked about was the absence of sidewalks in residential areas that were developed during the past several decades. I contend that the decades-long loss of sidewalks in neighborhoods has negatively affected the American family.)

A Broken Hip Episode

The rehab experience continued to percolate in my mind. It had nothing to do with the staff at the Willows, who had been a pleasure to know and who had done their best to compensate for a shortage of personnel and long hours. I knew there were far worse places and had experienced one after a knee surgery a couple of years before. I'd even chosen it because, if I remember correctly, it had been recommended by an orthopedic doctor.

Left there at some hour close to noon, a day or so after surgery, my arrival went unacknowledged for several hours while the staff and patients got through lunch and whatever else was going on. The people from the hospital knew what room number I'd been assigned and had quickly put me there before their departure. No interest was evident on the part of rehab staff and certainly there was no lunch offered.

Rehabilitation work was done in a too-small facility with too-few therapists using too little equipment and eventually someone got around to telling me that since it was Friday there would be no therapy for me. Nor was there any on Saturday and Sunday. Three days shot, I thought, sure that some entity was being billed for my presence, despite a lack of interest on the part of management and staff.

On Monday, Tuesday and Wednesday, therapy was either cut short or skipped. Meals that would later make the Willows look like a gourmet establishment came and went. Actually, they might have come but didn't get far when time came to take them away. When several trays with partly-eaten food ended up in the bathroom, lined up on the floor, Patty and I agreed that it was time I signed out.

It still causes me sorrow to think there were people who, for one reason or another, had to be in that place. The memory makes me wonder if some of the people who die after they've broken a hip have done so when in a place like that.

Actually, I have a number of friends who live, permanently, in nicer places that have several levels of superior care. They had opted to spend senior years in them, buying in at great cost to have houses or apartments or rooms where they can live independently while choosing whether or not to have meals in communal dining rooms and whether to participate in other amenities. Over time, as a resident required more care, there would be further services.

A friend broke her shoulder in a fall at a downtown restaurant and spent a number of pleasant weeks in an on-campus rehab facility until she was

A Broken Hip Episode

better. An acquaintance suffered a serious mental decline and was admitted to an on-campus department for continuing care.

Envy is not one of my character flaws but I am regretful that, should the time come when I can't live at home, I won't have the financial wherewithal for such a place. More than that, I mourn that such facilities exist only for those with excellent financial resources who can come up with hundreds of thousands of dollars. As far as I know, there are no official statistics to prove yea or nay but I'd be willing to bet that people with broken hips seldom die in places like that. Still, keeping an open mind works for all situations and, publicity to the contrary, bad experiences no doubt occur at all levels of affluence.

Both ends of the care center spectrum exist in every town and state in the United States, although some states have a more acceptable percentage of good care centers than others. North Carolina, where I live, is one of the worst. Several states have twice as many good ones as the Carolinas but in no state in the country are much more than 50 % of its care centers regarded as truly acceptable. (AARP, March 2018.)

Like politics, this is a subject that needs to be talked about and I began asking questions and looking for books. Let me tell you, there aren't many books. People who are young or even middle age, seldom give care centers a thought unless they have relatives in one and a lot of the elderly cross their fingers in the hope that they'll never need one. Insurance policies that were sold to take care of such needs are too expensive for most folks and, in actuality, the policies are getting more and more iffy.

There are thousands of verbal stories as relatives and friends recall what happened to a parent or some other relative who had to, at last, take up residence in a care center for the aged. Rarely, have such placements been a welcome choice but the aged often need more attention, sometimes around the clock, than families can provide. Then, once in a care center, new problems arise. Food may be unpalatable so the patient stops eating. Medications can be delayed or misused or skipped entirely. A staff person may be abusive. The patient may dwindle away from the lack of social interaction.

One of my friends recalled a time when she had worked in the office of a nursing home that did many things wrong but spent money on the appearance of the facility. "Don't go by how a place looks," she says. "Nursing home owners know that the public looks at pretty lobbies and nicely carpeted halls. It's

A Broken Hip Episode

the same as judging a book by its cover."

She recalls, as well, that when her mother died—after many months in a care center following a broken hip—one of the causes of death listed on the certificate was "malnutrition."

Unlike politics, care centers are not a stimulating topic, and the two entities never meet. I've certainly never encountered or read about a politician who's included better care centers in her/his platform.

Come to think of it, it would probably be a "her" because it's mostly women who end up sacrificing their own time and opportunity in order to care for the elderly who have more needs than money.

There was a time, a number of years back, when the care industry got excited about something called an "Eden" movement wherein centers included animals, birds, and lots of plants. The Willows had been one of the places that had tried it out but had given it up. On Friday evenings now, a few people walk their dogs through and patients are allowed to pet them for a moment or so if they wish, which is nice. When I was there, there was an artificial plant in my room that required no attention at all and stood in a corner gathering dust. I suppose that was one of the things that had gone wrong with the Eden movement; living things require attention and things that require attention need staff people to attend to them. Whoops! There go the profits!

In mid-August, our household had an addition. Grandson Phillip does volunteer work at a nearby animal shelter, working with dogs that are available for adoption. We, especially Patty, found that of great interest. She looked back with pleasure and nostalgia at times past when there had been a dog in her family and sometimes went online to look at descriptions of various breeds.

I, too, had dogs when the children were still at home and had loved them. For many recent years, however, I'd had a beautiful Maine Coon cat, Chi, that I'd adored. Sadly, Chi had died the year before my broken hip episode and I still mourned her.

But time had passed and, given my druthers, not to mention how relatively easy it is to share a household with a cat, I'd have been delighted to have another one—but my sense of fair play told me that it was time Patty got her dog. She had had a Lab and another large mix in time past but didn't want a big one this time around so we looked online at smaller breeds—a King Charles spaniel or a cock-a-poo. "I don't want a puppy," she said. "They're too much work."

A Broken Hip Episode

Phillip enquired one evening if we'd be interested in fostering a dog from the shelter. There are some that, for one reason or another, were not yet available for adoption but would benefit from spending time in a family home before their problem was totally solved.

"What do you think, Mom?" said Pat. I didn't give it a lot of thought. The rest of the family wanted to do it and I wanted them to be happy.

"Okay," I said. "If a dog we foster turns out to be difficult, it can just be returned to the shelter, right?"

Several days later, Phillip came home with a six-month-old puppy. It was smallish, an animal shelter special that was purported to be a beagle—or beagle*ish* at least. His name was Franklin and he suffered from allergies or asthma or something of the sort. In two weeks he would be neutered and put up for adoption, but he'd benefit from being in a home for the interim. Happily, he had either been housebroken or had trained himself.

Franklin was quiet and sweet. When he was overcome by his allergy, he rolled on the floor, sneezing, and our hearts went out to him. Despite his problem, he never had an accident, waiting until he could get out into our fenced backyard for his considerable number of excretions. He contentedly ate the puppy food that the shelter sent home with him and snuggled when he was petted. Did any dog ever have a nicer disposition? As a beagle, he fit into the category we'd been looking at online.

One week later, we were called by the folks at the shelter, asking us to return Franklin because he was going to be neutered in a couple of days, after which he'd go into the area for dogs available for adoption.

We were saddened by that, not quite ready to give him up. "He has such a nice personality," we said to one another. "Should we—you know—think of adopting him?" He wasn't quite one of the elegant breeds that we'd looked at, online, but he was so *nice!* Besides, he had this short brown fur that wouldn't require all the grooming that a more stylish breed would require.

Franklin had his surgery and was on the market two days later when Patty, with my endorsement, went over to the animal shelter, paid the adoption fee and brought him home.

Our experience with other pets had taught us that superior nutrition results in superior outcomes so Patty went hunting for the best grain-free puppy food on the market and found it—at elevated prices. Franklin began proving the wisdom of her decision within days.

A Broken Hip Episode

A fairly small dog at six months, he began growing. And growing. His legs began to lengthen to a point where we had to say, "There's some terrier in there, don't you think?" This opinion was accelerated when Franklin demonstrated a talent for walking around on his hind legs and posing at attention, his front legs at ease, chest level. We'd seen the like at circus events. He sneezed only rarely, causing us to wonder if he'd had an allergy to the grains in the food he'd been fed in earlier months.

And still he grew. His short hair gathered into balls of fuzz that rolled across our hardwood floors, requiring constant flourishes of a broom and dust mop. He had some separation anxiety that was apparent in his refusal to stay out in the fenced-in yard unless one of us was with him and he had a tendency to poop in the house in protest when one of us left.

No longer the quiet, sweet little dog he had been when we first got to know him, he was, instead, a happy-go-lucky personality that was dedicated to the pleasures of family life. His heritage might be questionable, but he had the beagle personality. If he had the least mean streak, it was never in evidence. He loved his toys more than any dog we'd ever known and was determined to be played with whenever he wasn't napping. He couldn't be cured of jumping on whomever he took a fancy to and, in fact, seemed immune to any kind of training.

In short, Franklin was a pistol, a moving definition of the word *puppy,* and we had months and months, a year and a half at least, before this dynamo would perhaps settle down to more serene adulthood.

In mid-August, Patty had to return to a new school year, leaving well before 8:00 in the morning and returning sometime after 5:00. Phillip, as well, had a schedule that often took him away from home until after 6:00 in the evening.

Franklin and I, left at home, began a period of hellish interaction. He chewed on and scratched up everything in sight.

Then he got into my bedroom one day when I hadn't closed the door tightly and ate my blue mesh shoes.

September, One Year Post Episode

One year after the hip break episode found me still hobbling but in general good health. In case I had any compulsion to do fall cleaning, it fell by the wayside.

OCD traits don't hold up well if one is old and recovering from a broken hip. They don't hold up at all if there's a puppy in the house that has its own ideas about how to spend time. Life with Franklin was hell on décor. Lamp cords had to be unplugged and out of reach. Likewise books, magazines, and other paper products in addition to sofa cushions and rugs had to be sequestered far from the scene of action. Franklin used his ability to balance on his hind legs to take things from end tables and windowsills that caught his interest (not including food because we were committed to never feeding him at mealtime or letting him eat anything but dog food). There were training books that I had ordered from online vendors and read obsessively and those were demolished immediately if I were careless about laying them down on a table beside an easy chair. He did an especially thorough number on a book by Cesar Millan (the "*Dog Whisperer*"), ripping off the cover and successive pages as if he entirely disapproved of the man's philosophy of dog rearing. I didn't whisper when I found the mess.

Kitchen curtains that had to be washed, ironed and rehung no longer fit into our lifestyle. Besides, I'd promised my several therapists that I'd never again stand on anything to get at something else. The curtains would have to be replaced by something easier to live with.

Franklin was in command and I wasn't happy about it.

Sometimes, I yelled at him. Never, ever did I swat him, though I longed to do so. He decided he didn't wish to be trained and that was that. We spent an inordinate amount of time in the fenced back yard where he would kindly bring me slobbery balls to throw for his amusement—for as long as I was willing to keep it up.

I grew depressed and knew I was going to have to get over it because all of us loved our naughty pup and giving him up would have broken our hearts. In the meanwhile, I lived for the hour toward evening when Patty came home from school and I spent a lot of time in my room with the door closed when she or Phillip was available to take over. Phillip's deep voice and experience at handling all kinds of dogs at

A Broken Hip Episode

the animal shelter meant that Frankie would behave respectfully with him. Patty, like me, had to contend with Franklin's enthusiastic petitions for attention and discovered that a few beans in an empty water bottle could, if rattled, get Frankie to cease and desist his wild puppy behavior, at least momentarily. He adored her and loved the leash-training walks that she took him on so much that the word "w a l k" had to be spelled out—until he learned, quite soon, how to translate the spelling into practical results.

One saving grace was that whenever I was on the computer, which meant that my back was turned to everything but the screen, Franklin would lie behind me, snoozing or at peace with his world. And that blessed fact means that I can write as much and whenever I please. I'm not sure why he does that. I've heard that the magic is in being turned away from the dog, with no eye contact going on. Also, I've learned to write while peering around the waste basket that stands on my desk, between me and the computer screen, out of the way of Franklin's desire to pull out and chew up whatever he finds in it. It's a small price to pay for freedom from puppy despotism.

By now, Trump and his assortment of appointees were six months into his term of office and it was as bad as I'd feared it would be. At least, there was a huge number of the press that reported every day's distressful events and those reports ended up in every publication that I encountered. I was grateful for that since I'd lived through and studied enough world events to know that a country is doomed when the press is stifled.

I continued to think about the inadequacies of care centers like the Willows or the institution from hell where I'd once gone after a new knee replacement. Unbecomingly nosy when I heard about a friend or a relative of a friend who was caught up in one of those places, I tended to share my thoughts and encourage their family to be alert.

There was a winter season coming up and that would require more time spent indoors trying to be a useful family member, not a fiend who spent hours yelling at a pup that wished to be let in and out, in and out. A likely pleasant October was going to be followed by four to five months of irksome weather changes. Did I have the stamina to face it?

It was time for some old fashioned self-confrontation. I'd better *find* the necessary endurance if I cared about my family and had a scrap of self-respect.

A Broken Hip Episode

Eighteen Month Report: It Is What It Is

One and a half years ago, I stepped backward from a stool when hanging curtains and changed my life.

No matter what I did or didn't do, my life would have changed anyway, because I am almost ninety years old and not likely to be, at best, very sprightly. Last September I walked better than I do now, but that's pretty much my own fault for neglecting to steadily perform the exercises that were pressed upon me by therapists all along the path since my fall.

I wall and furniture surf often, particularly during the first hour of each day. Generally, the unsteadiness of the early morning gives way to more stability and if the weather is reasonable I can get in my car and drive to the grocery store or a medical appointment or a meeting.

Scarlett, my red walking stick, goes most places with me, although she stays in my car when I get home. In the house, I get along without a cane or stick but by evening I'm hobbling quite a lot more than I was earlier in the day. When the weather warms up, I'll coax Patty into taking me along when she walks Franklin. Franklin isn't a very dependable walker, either, since he feels obligated to chase every squirrel that crosses his field of vision. At least I don't do that.

There isn't going to be any more spring or fall cleaning of the kind I did most of my adult life. Nevertheless, there are satisfactions to tackling a single chore—a closet for example, culling the items that can/should be given away or thrown away and tidying the rest for better access. There are endless numbers of these potential projects.

I take my turn at cooking dinner, doing dishes, sweeping the kitchen, and other routine chores. I've reluctantly come to realize that I'm quite slow at these things but that, most of the time, it doesn't matter.

Franklin has requirements and if nobody else is around to fulfill them, he happily allows me to let him in and out, in and out, and doesn't complain about the way I throw his tennis balls. He regularly assists my writing by curling up under my feet or behind me when I'm writing, only occasionally reminding me that I keep the best doggie treats in the house at my desk and that he is entitled to one *right now*. He has brought tremendous joy to our lives, even when being a pain in the neck, and his presence disallows any tendency for someone who has had a broken hip episode to get bogged down in pessimistic brooding.

A Broken Hip Episode

Donald Trump has now been the President of the United States for over a year and he is an undeniable disaster. The whole world is watching him and at times when I haven't kept track of a particularly terrible scenario, someone else has done so and worried aloud about heading him off at the gap. There is comfort in this universal awareness and a bit of hope that upcoming elections will at least make Congress and the judiciary aware that a lot of us are mad as hell and aren't going to take it anymore.

My continuing concern is about care centers. An AARP publication in spring 2018 indicated the percentage of acceptable care centers in each state and quite a few, including North Carolina, rated badly. No state in the country had a rating much above fifty percent and common sense says that of the well-rated, a significant number are probably in the "too costly for the average person" category. A hopeful editorial admitted that attention must be paid and, in the future, perhaps that will be the case. In the meanwhile, I grit my teeth when I read that Care Center X is being purchased by another entity that already owns several. They are planning to make a profit from the dollars paid by or on behalf of poor sick people.

A 2017 book (*Being Mortal,* Gawande) comes closer than any other book I've encountered to being written in layman language that spells out what it is to age and the difficulties faced by the elderly and their families in coping with available resources. The author has plenty to say about care centers and says that more attention is being paid to negative places and that there will be a trend toward better ones in the future.

Again, to quote my Jewish in-laws, "his word in God's ear."

I haven't, other than Gawande's book heard anything much that allows me to believe in his optimism. I hope the AARP follows up because they have access to so many entities.

During spring vacation, Patty and I went to visit our local animal shelter that was redesigned to be pretty much state of the art. Franklin came to us from that facility so we were especially pleased about its roomy facilities for both cats and dogs. There are many volunteers, some big and strong enough to handle unexpected scenarios and all with kind voices and nurturing ways. Some of the animals have suffered deprivation and illness and the professional staff knows what to do in those cases so the animal

A Broken Hip Episode

will have a better quality of life. Frankie is probably a shining example of their skill.

When we left the shelter, it was with light hearts and speculations as to which animal we might have adopted if Franklin hadn't joined our family a few months before.

But it didn't take long before I realized the contrast between that animal shelter and the way too many care centers for the elderly are run. The shelter is a proud municipal home for animals that need care. There is a dedicated staff and a healthy supply of volunteers and nobody—*nobody*—cutting corners so that somebody can make a profit.

If it had been a care center like those for people, it might have looked impressive in the lobby but the food might have been so unappealing that a lot of animals wouldn't have wanted to eat it or so lacking in nutrition that it didn't promote health and healing. There would have been fewer caregivers and little incentive for engaging volunteers. The animals would be awakened at odd hours of the night to receive pills and shots and would all have to be awake and ready for the day at precisely the same time in the morning. They would droop from a lack of socializing and soon curl up in apathy.

So that is a major point I took away from my

broken hip episode—that care centers are a significant concern that most of us ignore until our life moves on to a time when we no longer can do so. I fell backward from a stool and broke my hip. No amount of exercise will lengthen the leg that is now shorter than the other and no effort will stop me from hobbling for the rest of my life.

Nevertheless, life is good despite changes. I have the utmost gratitude for my family's love and care. Franklin is heaven-sent. Who else but a rambunctious puppy can so efficiently make one forget the stuff that deserves to be forgotten?

Is this state of affairs permanent? No, of course not. If one is eighty-nine and lucky, it is a certainty that ninety is what will follow.

A crazy puppy eventually turns into a pleasantly mature adult dog.

There is no guarantee that one won't have more serious falls. Despite all the wall surfing and walking and avoidance of obsessive-compulsive hanging of curtains, one may still end up with additional broken bones.

Come to think of it, I don't really feel bad about all that or particularly scared. I will try very hard to stay upright but there are no guarantees. That's the great thing about aging; the time is past for thinking of things one should have done and obsessing about what may happen. A good book, a chat with a good friend or beloved family member—plus a comfortable chair—are sufficient unto the day.

Oh—one more thing. As long as you draw breath, don't forget to vote.

www.ingramcontent.com/pod-product-compliance
Lightning Source LLC
Chambersburg PA
CBHW070849050426
42453CB00012B/2106